TRUMP:
THE BUILDING OF AN EMPIRE

TRUMP:
THE BUILDING OF AN EMPIRE

JHON DOOLEY

A Critic's Choice paperback
from Lorevan Publishing, Inc.
New York, New York

ISBN: 1-55547-262-1

First Critic's Choice edition: August, 1988

From LOREVAN PUBLISHING, INC.

Published in association with GAP International.

Critic's Choice Paperbacks
31 E. 28th St.
New York, New York 10016

Manufactured in the United States of America

Dedication

I'd like to thank the following people for their help, support and inspiration.

First, I must thank my beautiful wife Elizabeth and my lovely daughter Andee Elizabeth, for their gracious patience and unfaltering support.

My special thanks to these people: Gary Noar, Bruce S. Cirlin of Dillinger Coach/Gaines limousines, Mr. Paul Kullman of the World Affairs Council, J.T. Hunn; CLU. Value Added Insurance Services, Charles and Ruth Holden, Peter Horner, Gary Brodsky of GAP International, David Brattstrom and Dawne Trent, Dale Tribue, the Eatery staff in Trinidad, Computers Plus & Kangaroo Software, L. J. Elder and Don Chin, Mario Celotto, Humbolt Brewery, Chris & Jerri, and extra special thanks go to Mr. Donald John Trump, for doing what he does so well.

"Playing God is a very difficult role. That's the ultimate role, and I'm not sure that I'd be up to that . . ."

—Donald J. Trump, 1988—

Introduction

Donald J. Trump. The name stands for achievement, vision, and power. To some, the name strikes a chord of fear, resounding through the levels of high finance. To others, Donald Trump is the icon of a generation. A corporate visionary, with the abilities to achieve where others would have certainly failed.

"There is no one my age who has accomplished more," Mr. Trump once said. "Everyone can't be the best."

He has built some of the world's greatest architectural achievements, and saved the fate of existing ones with insight and ingenuity. He has been called the master of the deal, and lived up to it.

Donald Trump is a fascinating and richly talented man. His business exploits are reported almost daily in the world's major media sources, and for good reason. He always seems to do the impossible. At times his persona exudes such excitement that you can't help but to share in it. Even when one has doubts, he moves, he adapts and succeeds. When he discovers a ripe deal in the making, he moves like the tip of a jet. Yet once committed, he has no problem taking the time to do the very best that is possible.

Donald Trump is an example that true excellence is still a living part of the American business ethic. And he's rich.

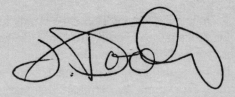

Chapter 1
Fred C. Trump, The Father of the Empire

"Donald is the smartest person I know . . . He has great vision, and everything he touches seems to turn to gold."

—Fred C. Trump—

Fred Trump became head of his family's household at the tender age of 11, when his alcoholic father died unexpectedly. Being the oldest male in a family of three that included his mother Elizabeth, he took charge and began to support them. Fred was always captivated by the complexities and process of the building and real estate industry. He made a point of attending late night carpentry and construction classes at his local high school. Fred began building soon after, and by the age of 16 had already built his first structure, a two-car garage for a neighborhood friend. The garage building job was such a success that he began a small business enterprise making them.

In 1922, Fred Trump made the difficult decision of not going to college, after graduating from high school. He chose to work, instead, as a carpenter's apprentice in Queens, New York, to better provide for his late father's family.

In his popular best-selling autobiography, *Trump; The Art of the Deal*, Donald Trump spoke of his father's varied and plentiful talents during the early beginnings of a career which eventually spawned a billion dollar company. "He was better with his hands than most," Mr. Trump wrote, "but he also had some other advantages. For starters, he was just a very smart guy. Even to this day," the youthful real estate mogul said, "he can add five columns of numbers in his head and keep them all straight. Between his night courses and his basic common sense, he was able to show the other carpenters, most of whom had no education at all, shortcuts, such as how to frame a rafter with a steel square."

Fred Trump's abilities brought him higher and higher in his field, as other workers slowly plodded ahead and stayed relatively inert. His progression quickened almost weekly, and he did his best to maintain a healthy fed household, while still being a very young man. The Trump ability to achieve at a very young age wasn't exclusive to

Fred Trump. Son Donald was a millionaire, by his own accord, when he was under thirty.

"In addition," Donald continued, "my father was always very focused and very ambitious. Most of his co-workers were happy to just have a job. My father not only wanted work, he also wanted to do well and to get ahead. Finally, my father just plain loved working. From as early as I can remember, my father would say to me, 'The most important thing in life is to love what you're doing, because that's the only way you'll be really good at it.' "

A year after Fred Trump graduated from high school, he built his first home. It was a one-family house, in Woodhaven, Queens, for less than $5,000. Fred was still not yet of age, so he formed his construction company under the banner of "Elizabeth Trump & Son" and had his mother sign checks and other legal documents. Elizabeth Trump & Son prospered for some time, and Fred Trump built home after home in communities like Queens Village, Hollis, and Woodhaven. The people who bought the homes were working-class, and they ate up the inexpensive brick, suburban type of home that Fred Trump offered. Accustomed to crowded and cramped apartments, the buyers relished the thought of having more space of their own. Soon expanding into much larger homes aimed toward a more affluent market, Fred Trump built a variety of Tudor-style, Victorian, and Colonial abodes.

This gave him time to organize his thoughts as the market for expensive homes dwindled, and he turned his attentions to a relatively new concept in shopping: the self-service supermarket. Fred Trump took the money he had made on the purchase of a bankrupt mortgage-service company, and built a supermarket equipped with all types of commercial tradesmen. Offering such services as butchering, tailoring, shoe repair and others, the market became an instant success. Fred sold the enterprise within a year for a substantial profit, in order to return to his first love, building.

He began building, after the depression's end, in the Flatbush area of Brooklyn. Success was at hand once again for Fred Trump, for the need for housing was immense. He sold seventy-eight homes in less than a month, and according to Donald Trump, ''during the next dozen years, he built 2,500 more throughout Queens and Brooklyn.''

Fred C. Trump met with good fortune once again in Mary Macleod, and the two were married in 1936. Fred's well earned fortune made it possible to send his brother John to college. Eventually, with the financial assistance of his brother, John Trump became a professor of physics. Fred was more than glad to assist John academically, and give him the proper education Fred had been forced to miss.

THE BUILDING OF AN EMPIRE

By 1946, Fred Trump had established himself as a capable and professional builder. He and his wife Mary had two children, Maryanne and Fred, Jr., and they were soon expecting their third child. Fred's peers had already accepted him as a leader in New York low and middle class housing. He was featured in a 1945 issue of *Professional Builder*, because of his new type of row housing. "At the present time," the article began, "he (Fred Trump) is working on a project of 1,000 home units in Bensonhurst on the New York Harbor.

"Much of his success as a producer of mass housing is timing the sequence of the operations of the various crafts on the job, knowing in advance what you are going to do and being ready to do it at the proper time. Another important factor, says Mr. Trump, 'is not to be found in methods or use of up-to-date equipment (as they are becoming standard on most jobs) but in getting the materials on time.'

"To accomplish this at the present time, Mr. Trump has a number of expediters in various locations whose sole job is to speed delivery of materials.

"As Mr. Trump sees it, the row or attached houses he is building are a 'halfway station between living in an apartment and a detached house. People living in these,' he says, 'will become educated to fit themselves for ownership of detached homes.' Trump has injected architectural appeal into these houses that takes them out of the ordinary class." *Professional Builder* chose to rerun the article on Fred Trump in the fiftieth anniversary issue of April, 1986. The editors of *Professional Builder* consider Fred Trump to be one "of the builders who made lasting contributions to housing." He also made a lasting contribution to the world of high profile real estate and corporate gamble that year; in 1946; Fred and Mary Trump gave birth to their third child, Donald John Trump.

Donald was born in a twenty-three-room house in Jamaica Estates, Queens, which his father Fred Trump had built.

"It's in his genes," said Fred Trump, in an article from *The New York Times Magazine*, explaining Donald Trump's real estate success, and his son's experience on the construction sites and in rental offices.

"Donald Trump is the Michael Jackson of real estate," says Irving Fisher of HRH Construction, N.Y. "We've been dealing with him since he was 16. He was on old trooper at age 25."

The article titled, "The Expanding Empire of Donald Trump," reads, "Some have said that his father's money and political contacts with the Brooklyn Democratic Organization, which produced former Mayor Abraham D. Beame and former Gov. Hugh L. Carey, are an important part of Donald Trump's success formula. To be sure, they played a part in his gaining a foothold in Manhattan real estate a decade ago (1974). 'It's good know know people,' Fred Trump told his son.''

William Geist wrote that ''His (Donald Trump's) success also derives from his marketing skills. 'I want to bring a little showmanship to real estate,' Mr. Trump says. He is often compared to the late William Zeckendorf, the renowned New York builder, who was said to owe much of his success to his personal flair. Other New York developers—including the Lefraks, the Rudins, the Tishmans, the Fishers, the Roses—go quietly about building more buildings than does Donald Trump, making their millions and keeping their names out of things.''

Donald Trump recalls his childhood household, and his father's strong influence on the Trump family. ''My father was the power and the bread-winner, and my mother was the perfect housewife. That didn't mean she sat around playing bridge and talking on the phone. There were five children in all, and besides taking care of us, she cooked and cleaned and darned socks and did charity work at the local hospital. We lived in a large house, but we never thought of ourselves as rich kids. We were brought up to know the value of a dollar and to appreciate the importance of hard work. Our family was always very close, and to this day they are my closest friends. My parents had no preten-tions. My father still works out of a small, modest back office on Avenue Z in the Sheepshead Bay section of Brooklyn, in a building he put up in 1948. It's simply never occurred to him to move.''

Donald always speaks highly of his father, and every other member of his family for that matter, because he got to experience his father's dextrous abilities first hand. By accompanying Fred to construction sites and acquired properties, Donald found the makings of himself in his intelligent and talented father. "You made it in my father's business,'' says the 42-year-old Donald, "—rent-controlled and rent-stabilized buildings—by being very tough and relentless. To turn a profit, you had to keep your costs down, and my father was always very price-conscious.

"He'd negotiate just as hard with a supplier of mops and floor wax as he would with the general contractor for the larger items on a project. One advantage my father had was that he knew what everything cost. No one could put anything over on him. If you know, for example, that a plumbing job is going to cost the contractor $400,000, then you know how far you can push the guy. You're not going to try to negotiate him down to $300,000, because that's just going to put him out of business. But you're also not going to let him talk you into $600,000.

"The other way my father got contractors to work for a good price was by selling them on his reliability. He'd offer a low price for a job, but then he'd say, 'Look, with me you get paid on time, and with someone else, who knows if you ever see your money?' He'd also point out that with him they'd get in and out quickly and on to the next job. And finally, because he was always building, he could hold out the promise of plenty of future work. His arguments were usually compelling.

"My father was also an unbelievably demanding taskmaster. Every morning at six, he'd be there at the site and he would just pound and pound and pound. He was almost a one man show. If a guy wasn't doing his job the way my father thought it should be done—and I mean any job, because he could do them all—he'd jump in and take over."

Donald recalls a reoccurring theme in the building of some of his father's projects. "It was always amusing to watch a certain scenario repeat itself. My father would start a building in, say, Flatbush, at the same time that two competitors began putting up their own buildings nearby. Invariably, my father would finish his building three or four months before his competitors did. His building would also be a little better looking then the other two, with a nicer, more spacious lobby and larger rooms in the apartments themselves. He'd rent them out quickly, at a time when it wasn't so easy to rent. Eventually, one or both of his competitors would go bankrupt before they'd finished their buildings, and my father would step in and buy them out. I saw this over and over."

*　　*　　*

When Donald was three years old, his father started building the first of many relatively large apartment complexes, which according to Donald made him, "one of the biggest landlords in New York's outer boroughs.

"Because he built the projects so efficiently," Donald wrote in his autobiography, "my father did exceptionally well with them. At the time, the government was still in the business of financing lower- and middle-income housing. To build Shore Haven," (which was the very first of Fred Trump's large apartment complexes), "for example, my father got a loan of $10.3 million from the Federal Housing Administration (FHA). The loan was based on what the agency projected as a fair and reasonable cost for the project, including a builder's profit of 7.5 percent.

"By pushing his contractors very hard, and negotiating hard with his suppliers, my father was able to bring the project in ahead of schedule and almost $1 million under budget. The term 'windfall profits' was actually coined to describe what my father and some others managed to earn through hard work and competence. Eventually such profits were disallowed.

"In the mean time, however, my father put up thousands of good quality lower- and middle-income apartments of the sort that no one is building today because it's not profitable and government subsidies have been eliminated. To this day, the Trump buildings in Queens and Brooklyn are considered among the best reasonably priced places to live in New York.''

It is more than apparent that Donald Trump gained a wealth of experience and knowledge from his father. Though he has broken new ground, and exploded from the modest beginnings of Fred Trump, Donald still carries the early memories with him, in the high profile, high society life he now leads.

In a cover-story report by writers Bill Powell and Peter McKillop in *Newsweek*, Fred Trump's constant influence on son Donald was briefly mentioned. ''Fred Trump, 83, still goes to work every day at his modest office in Brooklyn. He got rich years ago building thousands of brick . . . homes for the emerging middle-class in Brooklyn and Queens. Fred talks to his son (Donald) nearly every day and says he is awed by what Donald's done. His son is still very much a product of the Brooklyn office. His vernacular is neither that of an aristocrat nor of a polished executive. That may be why today, despite the outrageous trappings of his wealth and the unyielding ambition, Donald Trump remains a rather familiar figure.''

Donald is then compared to a character in a prize winning play called ''Glengarry Glen Ross,'' which is described as, ''a slick, street-smart real estate salesman named Ricky Roma.'' The authors of the article ask that you "forget" Roma, and that you substitute Donald Trump for the central character, who says, "I do those things which seem correct to me *today*. I trust myself. And if security concerns me, I do that which *today* I think will make me secure. And every day I do that, and when that day arrives that I need a reserve, a) odds are that I have it, and b) the *true* reserve that I have is the strength that I have of *acting each day* without fear, according to the dictates of my mind. Stocks, bonds, objects of art, real estate. Now: what are they? An opportunity. To what? To make money? Perhaps. To *lose* money? Perhaps. To 'indulge' and to 'learn' about ourselves? Perhaps. So fucking *what*? What *isn't*? They're an *opportunity*. That's all. They're an *event*. A guy comes up to you, you make a call, you send in a brochure, it doesn't matter. 'There're these *properties* I'd like you to see.' What does it mean? What you *want* it to mean . . ."

"For Trump," the writers added, "it can only mean more money, more power and—what his $1 billion ego seems to covet most—more attention."

Robert H. Boyle, in an article about Donald Trump which graced the pages of *Sports Illustrated*, says that the Trump story "reads like a saga by Thomas Mann.

"Donald Trump is of Swedish-German descent, but he says that many people think he's Jewish because his family owns so many buildings in

Brooklyn." In fact, Donald Trump was given an award in 1976 from the National Jewish Hospital in Denver. "He is one of five children born to Fred and Mary Trump, who live in Queens, across from the East River from Manhattan. . . . The master builder is Fred, whose own father died when he was 12" (though Donald Trump himself says that his grandfather died when Fred Trump was only eleven, in *Trump, The Art of the Deal*). "Now 78, Fred has a full head of red hair, a bristly mustache and an erect carriage.

" 'The chicks think I'm 50,' Fred Trump says, obviously delighted with his long lasting vigor.

"He spends his time in his office, at 600 Avenue Z in Brooklyn," Boyle wrote, "looking after his rental units. Manhattan is Donald's stomping ground, not his.

"After graduating from high school, Fred Trump went to work as a carpenter's helper. 'Learn a trade, and you can always go back to it if things go wrong,' he says. 'By the age of 20 he had built a one-family house in the Woodhaven section of Queens. In 1935, in the depths of the Depression, he put up 78 two-family houses in the Flatbush section of Brooklyn. Other developers had shied away because the area had been mined for sand and then filled with garbage, but Trump devised a way of putting in pilings to give the houses stable foundations, and he was off and running to a

15

fortune." A fortune that he shared with his sons Donald and Robert.

Fred Trump was as successful as a father as he proved to be as a real estate developer. The children led lives rich with spiritual and developmental lessons, with the financial earnings of Fred Trump as a bonus. The family members grew up in a very competitive atmosphere, and, therefore, each grew to know competitiveness. Fred Trump was still a relatively young man, with five intelligent children, and a loving compassionate wife. The Trump household was in many ways, a very traditional family. The Trumps practiced good and honest values, and to this day, the various members of the family have established themselves as straight forward, disciplined people. Maryanne Trump-Barry, the eldest of the five Trump children, worked her way up to become a United States federal court judge in New Jersey by first working for five years as a federal prosecutor, in the U.S. Attorney's office. Maryanne, who at first worked as a housewife, after graduating from Mount Holyoke College, returned to her law studies, after David (her son) was old enough to take care of himself. In Donald Trump's words, "Maryanne is really something." The other children. Fred, Jr. (who's unexpected death a few years ago at the age of forty-three stands as one of the few sad notes in the Trump saga), Robert, Donald, and Elizabeth, each had their own ideas, and their careers took diverse paths. Elizabeth Trump works at the renowned Chase Manhattan Bank in Manhattan. Brother Robert, who is an executive Vice President in Donald's company, The Trump Organization, is also well respected in the business world. Robert Trump is "very talented and effective" according to Donald, who holds obvious respect for him. The Trump family has always been very close, always keeping contact with each other, and consult one another often. Donald often asks Maryanne and her husband John Barry about legal options concerning a variety of questions he has about his many "deals."

Says Donald, "Maryanne is very smart, she obviously knows more about law than I do. Robert, who is two years younger than me," says the multimillionaire Donald, "is soft spoken and easygoing . . . I think it must be hard to have me as a brother, but he's never said anything about it and we're very close. He is definitely the only guy in my life whom I ever call 'honey.' Robert gets along with almost everyone, which is great for me since I sometimes have to be the bad guy."

Donald recalls the plight of his late brother, Fred Trump, Jr. "My older brother, Freddy, the first son, had perhaps the hardest time in our family. My father is a wonderful man, but he is also very much a business guy and strong and tough as hell. My brother was just the opposite. Handsome as he could be, he loved parties and had a great, warm personality and a real zest for life. He didn't have an enemy in the world. Naturally, my father very much wanted his oldest son in the business, but unfortunately, business just wasn't for Freddy. He went to work with my father reluctantly, and he never had a feel for real estate. He wasn't the kind of guy who could stand up to a killer contractor or negotiate with a rough supplier. Because my father was so strong, there were inevitable confrontations between the two of them. In most cases, Freddy came out on the short end.

"Eventually," Donald wrote, "it became clear to all of us that it wasn't working, and Freddy went off to pursue what he loved most—flying airplanes. He moved to Florida, became a professional pilot, and flew for TWA. He also loved fishing and boating. Freddy was probably happiest during that period in his life, and yet I can remember saying to him, even though I was eight years younger, 'Come on, Freddy, what are you doing? You're wasting your time.' I regret now that I ever said that.

"Perhaps I was just too young to realize that it was irrelevant what my father or I thought about what Freddy was doing. What mattered was that he enjoyed it. Along the way, I think Freddy became discouraged, and he started to drink, and that led to a downward spiral. At the age of forty-three, he died."

The scars that death leave on people are deep and everlasting. There is no soothing the regret, especially when that regret involves a loved one. Donald will probably take his feelings for his brother to the grave with him. "It's very sad," he recalls, "because he was a wonderful guy who never quite found himself. In many ways he had it all, but the pressures of our particular family were not for him. I only wish I had realized this sooner."

Though Donald denies that he was intimidated by his father, it is obvious that he maintains a proud respect for him; and for good reasons. Fred Trump helped him become what he is today. It is regrettable that Fred, Jr., didn't have the chance to reach his potential, but had he lived I'm sure he would share Donald's respect for Fred Trump. In most cases like Fred, Jr.'s, the blame is often placed upon the person's self, while feeling inadequate in the presence of a strong personality.

In an article by Judy Klemesrud, who accompanied Donald Trump during a "day in the life," she points out that though he feigns being intimidated by his father, some still shows through. "Mr. Trump, a glib, nonstop talker," Ms. Klemesrud wrote, "suddenly turned quiet when he stopped at the Trump Organization's headquarters, at 600 Avenue Z in Brooklyn, to consult with his father. Face to face, the son seemed affectionately intimidated by the older man." While more recently, Donald said, ". . . I was never intimidated by my father, the way most people were. I stood up to him, and he respected that. We had a relationship (while growing up) that was almost businesslike. I sometimes wonder if we'd have gotten along so well. if I hadn't been as business-oriented as I am.''

"I gave Donald free rein," Fred Trump said to Judy Klemesrud, in his Avenue Z office in 1976. "He has a great vision, and everything he touches seems to turn to gold. As long as he has this great energy in abundance, I'm glad to let him do it.''

"The most important influence on me, growing up, was my father, Fred Trump," Donald wrote in his autobiography. "I learned a lot from him. I learned about toughness in a very tough business, I learned about motivating people, and I learned about competence and efficiency: get in, get it done right, and get out.

"At the same time," he wrote, "I learned very early on that I didn't want to be in the same business my father was in. He did very well building rent-controlled and rent-stabilized housing in Queens and Brooklyn, but it was a very tough way to make a buck. I wanted to try something grander, more glamorous, and more exciting. I also realized that if I ever wanted to be known as more than Fred Trump's son, I was eventually going to have to go out and make my own mark. I'm fortunate that my father was content to stay with what he knew and did so well. That left me free to make my mark in Manhattan. Even so, I never forgot the lessons I learned at my father's side.''

Because of his father's influence on him, Donald says that he was, ''drawn to business very early.'' The young Donald Trump seemed as strong willed and aggressive as his father Fred. ''Even in elementary school,'' says Donald, ''I was a very assertive, aggressive kid. In the second grade I actually gave a teacher a black eye—I punched my music teacher because I didn't think he knew anything about music and I almost got expelled.'' It is a good thing for Donald's present day business associates, that today he uses different methods of persuasion. He has learned other ways of dealing with incompetence, and sees his early physical aggressiveness in a different light. ''I'm not proud of that,'' Donald recalls, ''but it's clear evidence that early on I had a tendency to stand up and make my opinions known in a very forceful way. The difference now is that I like to use my brain instead of my fists.

''I was always something of a leader in my neighborhood,'' Donald remembers. ''Much the way it is today, people either liked me a lot, or they didn't like me at all. In my own crowd I was very well liked, and I tended to be the kid that others followed. As an adolescent I was mostly interested in creating mischief, because for some reason I liked to stir things up, and I liked to test people. I'd throw water balloons, shoot spitballs, and make a ruckus in the schoolyard and at birthday parties. It wasn't malicious so much as it was aggressive. My bother Robert likes to tell the story of the time when it became clear to him where I was headed.'' In fact this short tale seems to be a favorite of newspaper columnists and magazine writers, too, as it appears in most every story about Donald Trump.

"One day,'' Donald fondly recalls, ''we were in the playroom of our house, building with blocks. I wanted to build a very tall building, but it turned out that I didn't have enough blocks. I asked Robert if I could borrow some of his, and he said, 'Okay, but you have to give them back when you're done.' I ended up using all of my blocks, and then all of his, and when I was done, I'd created a beautiful building. I liked it so much that I glued the whole thing together. And that,'' he says, ''was the end of Robert's blocks.''

Because of Donald's tendency to delight in various forms of creative mischief, Fred sent him to a strict military school to help iron out some of his unsocial activities. "I wasn't thrilled about the idea,'' Donald recalls, ''but it turned out he was right.

"Beginning in the eighth grade I went to the New York Military Academy in upstate New York. I stayed through my senior year, and along the way I learned a lot about discipline, and about channeling my aggression into achievement. In my senior year I was appointed a captain of the cadets.

"There was one teacher in particular who had a big impact on me," Donald once said. "Theodore Dobias was a former drill sergeant in the marines, and physically he was very tough and very rough, the kind of guy who could slam into a goalpost wearing a football helmet and break the post rather than his head. He didn't take any back talk from anyone, least of all from kids who came from privileged backgrounds. If you stepped out of line, Dobias smacked you and he smacked you hard. Very quickly I realized that I wasn't going to make it with this guy by trying to take him on physically. A few less fortunate kids chose that route, and they ended up getting stomped. Most of my classmates took the opposite approach and became nebbishes. They never challenged Dobias about anything.

"I took a third route, which was to use my head to get around the guy. I figured out what it would take to get Dobias on my side. In a way, I finessed him. It helped that I was a good athlete, since he was a baseball coach and I was a captain of the team. But I also learned how to play *him*.

"What I did," he says, "basically, was to convey that I respected his authority, but that he didn't intimidate me. It was a delicate balance. Like so many strong guys, Dobias had a tendency to go for the jugular if he smelled weakness. On the other hand, if he sensed strength but you didn't try to undermine him, he treated you like a man. From the time I figured that out—and it was more an instinct than a conscious thought—we got along great.

"I was a good enough student at the academy," Trump says, "although I can't say I ever worked very hard. I was lucky that it came relatively easily to me, because I was never all that interested in schoolwork. I understood early on that the whole academic thing was only a preliminary to the main event—which was going to be whatever I did after I graduated from college."

Trump's experience with the academic realities of college come forward in his memories of Fred Trump's lack of a formal education. "Perhaps because my father never got a college degree himself, he continued to view people who had one with a respect that bordered on awe. In most cases they didn't deserve it. My father could run circles around most academics, and he would have done very well in college, if he'd been able to go.

"Almost from the time I could walk, I'd been going to construction sites with my father. Robert and I would tag along and spend our time hunting for empty soda bottles, which we'd take to the store for deposit money. As a teenager, when I came home from school for vacation, I followed my father around to learn about the business close up—dealing with contractors or visiting buildings or negotiating for a new site.

"After I graduated from New York Military Academy in 1964, I flirted briefly with the idea of attending film school at the University of Southern California. I was attracted to the glamour of the movies, and I admired guys like Sam Goldwyn, Darryl Zanuck, and most of all Louis B. Mayer, whom I considered great showmen. But in the end I decided real estate was a much better business."

Donald Trump started his college training by attending Fordham University in the Bronx, so that he could live as close to home as possible. "I got along very well with the Jesuits who ran the school, but after two years, I decided that as long as I had to be in college, I might as well test myself against the best." A practice that he's continued to this day. Donald applied and was accepted to the Wharton School of Finance at the University of Pennsylvania. According to Mr. Trump, "At that time, if you were going to make a career in business, Wharton was the place to go. Harvard Business School may produce a lot of CEOs—guys who manage public companies—but the real entrepreneurs all seemed to go to Wharton: Saul Steinberg, Leonard Lauder, Ron Pearlman—the list goes on and on.

"Perhaps the most important thing I learned at Wharton was not to be overly impressed by academic credentials. It didn't take me long to realize that there was nothing particularly awesome or exceptional about my classmates, and that I could compete with them just fine. The other important thing I got from Wharton was a Wharton degree. In my opinion, that degree doesn't prove very much, but a lot of people I do business with take it very seriously, and it's considered very prestigious. So all things considered, I'm glad I went to Wharton.''

Donald Trump took his degree back home, and went to work full time for Fred Trump. Though he was now involved with the family business, he began to formulate his own ideas about what to do with his natural talent and scholastic abilities. ''I continued to learn a lot,'' Donald says, ''but it was during this period that I began to think about alternatives.

''For starters,'' he says, ''my father's scene was a little rough for my taste—and by that I mean physically rough. I remember, for example, going around with the men we called rent collectors. To do this job you had to be physically imposing, because when it came to collecting rent from people who didn't want to pay, size mattered a lot more than brains.'' Brains, however, were a much needed asset to those in the position of collection, as Donald soon learned. The combination of brain and brawn were necessary to stay alive.

''One of the first tricks I learned was that you never stand in front of someone's door when you knock. Instead, you stand by the wall and reach over to knock. The first time a collector explained that to me, 'What's the point?' I said. He looked at me like I was crazy. 'The point,' he said, 'is that if you stand to the side, the only thing exposed to danger is your hand.' I wasn't sure what he meant. 'In this business,' he said, 'if you knock on the wrong apartment at the wrong time, you're liable to get shot.'

"My father never sheltered me," Donald Trump says of his initial business with Fred Trump, "but even so, this was not a world I found attractive. I'd just graduated from Wharton, and suddenly here I was in a scene that was violent at worst and unpleasant at best. For example, there were tenants who'd throw their garbage out the window, because it was easier than putting it in the incinerator. At one point, I instituted a program to teach people about using the incinerators. The vast majority of tenants were just fine, but the bad element required attention, and to me it just wasn't worth it.

"The second thing I didn't find appealing was that the profit margins were so low. You had no choice but to pinch pennies, and there was no room for luxuries. Design was beside the point because every building had to be pretty much the same: four walls, common brick façades, and straight up. You used red brick, not necessarily because you liked it but because it was a penny a brick cheaper than tan brick."

Mr. Trump likes to recall his father's visit to

Trump Tower while it was still under construction, and his astonishment at his son's choice of expensive materials. Having seen the necessity of cutting corners in his own buildings, Fred Trump was concerned that son Donald was spending much too much on accessories that would probably go unnoticed anyway.

"I still remember the time when my father visited the Trump Tower site, midway through construction. Our façade was a glass curtain wall, which is far more expensive than brick. In addition, we were using the most expensive glass you can buy—bronze solar. My father took one look, and said to me, 'Why don't you forget about the damn glass? Give them four or five stories of it and then use common brick for the rest. Nobody is going to look up anyway.' It was a classic," Mr. Trump says happily. "Fred Trump standing there on 57th Street and Fifth Avenue trying to save a few bucks. I was touched, and of course I understood where he was coming from—but also exactly why I'd decided to leave.

"The real reason I wanted out of my father's business—more important than the fact that it was physically rough and financially tough—was that I had loftier dreams and visions. And there was no way to implement them building housing in the outer boroughs."

Donald Trump also credits his mother Mary, for many of his outstanding personal qualities. Never one to withhold credit where it is due, he reminisces about Mary Trump's affect on his adult life. "Looking back," he begins, "I realize now that I got some of my showmanship from my mother. She always had a flair for the dramatic and the grand. She was a very traditional housewife, but she also had a sense of the world beyond her. I still remember my mother, who is Scottish by birth, sitting in front of the television set to watch Queen Elizabeth's coronation and not budging for an entire day. She was just enthralled by the pomp and circumstance, the whole idea of royalty and glamour. I also remember my father that day, pacing around impatiently. 'For Christ's sake, Mary,' he'd say. 'Enough is enough, turn it off. They're all a bunch of con artists.' My mother didn't even look up. They were total opposites in that sense. My mother loves splendor and magnificence, while my father, who is very down-to-earth, gets excited only by competence and efficiency."

In a sense, Donald Trump is the perfect combination of Fred and Mary's outstanding qualities. He is a perfect example, that when oil and vinegar are mixed, you sometimes get a great salad dressing.

Chapter 2
The First Big Deals

". . . I got to know a lot of people when I moved to Manhattan, and I got to know properties, but I still couldn't find anything to buy at a price that I liked. Then, suddenly, in 1973 things began to turn bad in Manhattan. I'd always assumed the market would cool off, because everything runs in cycles and real estate is no different. Even so, I never expected things to get as bad as they did. It was a combination of factors. First, the federal government announced a moratorium on housing subsidies, which they had been giving out by the bushel, particularly in the city. At the same time, interest rates began to rise, after being so stable for so many years that it was easy to forget they could move at all. Then, to make things worse, there was a spurt of inflation, particularly in construction costs, which seem to rise even when there's no inflation anywhere else.

"But the biggest problem by far was with the city itself. The city's debt was rising to levels that started to make everyone very nervous. For the first time you heard people talk about the city going bankrupt. Fear led to more fear. Before long New York was suffering from a crisis of confidence. People simply stopped believing in the city."
—Donald Trump, in *Trump, the Art of the Deal*—

Donald Trump bought his first building complex in Cincinnati, Ohio, with financial assistance from his father. He was still in college, and even then he had a keen business sense. "In college," Mr. Trump wrote in his best-selling biography, "while my friends were reading comics and the sports pages of newspapers, I was reading the listings of FHA foreclosures. It might seem a bit abnormal to study lists of federally financed housing projects in foreclosure, but that's what I did. And that's how I found out about Swifton Village."

The development was a 1,200-unit apartment complex which was in trouble. The development had more than eight hundred empty apartments, the government had foreclosed on the property, and numerous other ills plagued it. In Trump's words, the place was "a disaster." From the buying eye though, that was a good incentive. The place was in such a wrecked condition that even with nationally distributed foreclosure journals' listings, Trump was the only interested party.

THE BUILDING OF AN EMPIRE

"My father and I put in a very minimal bid for Swifton," Mr. Trump began, "and it was accepted. We ended up paying less than $6 million for a job which had cost twice that much to build just two years earlier. We were also immediately able to get a mortgage for what we paid, plus about $100, which we put toward fixing the place up. In other words, we got the project without putting down any money of our own. All we had to do was go and run it. And if we did even a halfway decent job, we could easily cover our mortgage from the proceeds of the rent.

"The fact that it was such a big job appealed to my father and to me because it meant we could focus a lot of energy on it without feeling we were wasting our time. It takes almost the same amount of energy to manage 50 units as it does 1,200 —except that with 1,200 you have a much bigger upside.

"After we negotiated the deal, success became a matter of management and marketing. The challange was to get the place rented, and rented to good tenants who would stay there. The tenants who were living in the project when I took over had ripped the place apart. Many of them had come down from the hills of Kentucky. They were very poor and had seven or eight children, almost no possessions, and no experience living in an apartment complex. They crammed into one-room and two-room apartments, and their children went wild. They would just destroy the apartments and wreak havoc on the property.

"The tenants not only didn't care, many of them also didn't see fit to pay rent. If you pressed them, they had a tendency to take off. What we discovered is that to avoid paying rent, these people would rent a trailer, pull up in front of their apartments at one or two in the morning, and disappear into the night with all of their belongings. That was fine by me, but I wanted to make sure we got paid first. Our solution was to institute a 'trailer-watch.' We had someone on round-the-clock patrol.

"After we got rid of the bad tenants, we set about fixing the place up to attract a better element. That required a substantial investment, almost $800,000 by the time we were done, which was a lot of money in those days. But it was more than worth it. In New York the laws prevent you from getting fair increases even when you make improvements, but in Cincinnati we were immediately able to charge and get much higher rents for the apartments at Swifton Village.

"The first thing we did was invest in beautiful white shutters for the windows. That may not sound like a big deal, but what the shutters did was give a bunch of cold red brick buildings a feeling of warmth and coziness, which was important. It was also much more expensive than you'd guess, because you're talking about 1,200 units, each of which has eight to ten windows. The next thing we did was rip out the cheap, horrible aluminum front doors on the apartments and put up beautiful colonial white doors.

"I made sure the white complex was very clean and very well managed. As I said earlier, I've always had a personal thing about cleanliness, but I also believe it's a very good investment. For example, if you want to sell a car and you spend five dollars to wash and polish it and then apply a little elbow grease, suddenly you find you can charge an extra four hundred dollars—and get it. I can always tell a loser when I see someone with a car for sale that is filthy dirty. It's so easy to make it look better.

"It's no different in real estate. Well-maintained real estate is always going to be worth more than poorly maintained real estate. That's been less true during the past few years in New York, when there's been such a fever for real estate that people buy anything. But it's a mistake to be lulled by good times. Markets always change, and as soon as there's a downturn, cleanliness becomes a major value.

"We painted the hallways, we sanded and stained the floors, we kept the vacant apartments immaculately clean, and we landscaped the grounds. We also ran beautiful newspaper ads for the project—at a time when not many people in Cincinnati were advertising real estate. People came to check us out, and the word of mouth started getting good. Within a year, the buildings were 100 percent rented.''

Eventually, Donald Trump spent less and less time at Swifton Village. He had already gone through many managers, and had finally come across one who could handle the job. It was a tenant that Mr. Trump had befriended who suggested that Trump sell the project while he still could. The area surrounding Swifton was becoming worse. Trump realized that a person who actually lived there, would know the most about the neighborhood, and he set out to sell. Mr. Trump knew he couldn't maintain a high level clientele if it wasn't safe for them to walk the streets in broad daylight. Trump went to Swifton and stayed a few days riding around the area. Seeing that his friend was correct, Trump left the seething streets, and put the entire complex up for sale.

The Trumps had been able to turn the development into a profitable enterprise, and the rent roll, as he calls it, was about $700,000 a year. An offer was made to buy Swifton Village by the Prudent Real Estate Investment Trust. REIT was in the process of buying up any existing properties that were available to them, and they sent a young man out to inspect the Swifton complex. Donald Trump tells the tale best.

''It turned out that what he wanted to do more than anything was go out for lunch. He'd heard about this restaurant in downtown Cincinnati called the Maisonette, which was supposed to be one of the five best restaurants in the country. He really wanted to eat there, and when he called to say he was coming, he asked me to make a lunch reservation, I said fine.

"His flight came in a little late, about midday, and I met him, and I took him over to Swifton Village and showed him the job. We still had 100 percent occupancy at the time, and he wasn't interested in asking a lot of questions beyond that. He was anxious to get to the Maisonette. It took about an hour to get there from Swifton, and we ended up spending about three hours over lunch, which is the opposite of the way I normally work. If I'd had only one day to look over a big job like Swifton, I'd sure as hell skip lunch and spend my time learning everything I could about what I was thinking of buying.

"By the time we were done with lunch, it was almost four o'clock, and I had to take him to his plane. He returned to New York well fed and feeling great, and he strongly recommended going ahead with the purchase. He told his bosses that the area was wonderful and that Swifton was a great deal. They approved the sale. The price was $12 million—or approximately a $6 million profit for us. It was a huge return on a short-term investment.

"What happened next is that we signed a contract. By then, I could see the dark clouds clearly on the horizon. A lot of tenants had their leases coming up and weren't planning to renew. We put a clause in the contract of sale saying that all representations contained in it were as of the signing of the contract—not as of the closing, which is what's typically required. In other words, we were willing to represent that the project was 100 percent rented at the time of the contract signing, but we didn't want to make the promise at the time of closing, three or four months down the line.

"The other thing I did was to insist on a clause in the contract in which they'd close, or else pay a huge penalty. That was also very unusual, because in nearly every other deal, the buyer puts up a 10 percent deposit, and if he fails to close, all he forfeits is the deposit.

"Frankly, the Prudent people should have been more prudent. But, as I said, the REITs were hot to trot, and . . . they couldn't make deals fast enough. In the end, of course, it never pays to be in too much of a hurry. On the day we closed, there were dozens of vacant apartments."

Donald had always had his sights set on entering Manhattan, and in 1971, he actually made the move there. He bought an apartment, and began looking at the many real estate deals that were available. He began frequenting the better clubs, and since he now resided there, he got to meet more and more of Manhattan's upper-crust, yet he couldn't find a deal that fit his personality. Mr. Trump has said that at that time in Manhattan, "It wasn't an environment conducive to new real estate development.

"In the first nine months of 1973," he wrote, "the city issued permits for about 15,000 new apartments and single family homes in the five boroughs. In the first nine months of 1974, the number dropped to 6,000.

"I worried about the future of New York City, too," Trump contended, "but I can't say it kept me up nights. I'm basically an optimist, and frankly, I saw the city's trouble as a great opportunity for me. Because I grew up in Queens, I believed, perhaps to an irrational degree, that Manhattan was always going to be the best place to live—the center of the world. Whatever troubles the city might be having in the short term, there was no doubt in my mind that things had to turn around ultimately. What other city was going to take New York's place?

"One day, in the summer of 1973, I came across a newspaper story about the Penn Central Railroad, which was in the middle of a massive bankruptcy filing. This particular story said that the Penn Central trustees had hired a company headed by a man named Victor Palmieri to sell off the assets of the railroad. Among the assets, it turned out, were those abandoned yards in the west Sixties, as well as more yards in the west

Thirties. The deal Victor made with the Penn Central was that each time his company managed to find a buyer for an asset, he got a percentage of the sale.

"I had never heard of Victor Palmieri, but I realized immediately that he was someone I wanted to know. I called his representatives and said, 'Hello, my name is Donald Trump, and I'd like to buy the Sixtieth Street yards.' The simplest approach is often the most effective.

"I think they liked my directness and my enthusiasm. I hadn't built anything yet, but what I did have was the willingness to go after things that people in a better position than mine wouldn't have considered seeking."

Since Mr. Trump was getting himself into the world of the "big boys," it was time that he had a bona fide company. He decided to form what is now known as Trump Organization. According to Trump, "Somehow the word 'organization' made it sound much bigger. Few people knew that the Trump Organization operated out of a couple of tiny offices on Avenue Z in Brooklyn."

In a newly formed relationship between Donald Trump and Victor Palmieri, big ideas were turned into reality. Mr. Trump was in the process of promoting himself, so that he had more credibility. He launched press conferences and released information about his intentions with the run down rail yards. "The other thing I promoted," Mr. Trump said, "was our relationship with politicians, such as Abraham Beame, who was elected mayor of New York in November 1973. My father did belong to the same Democratic club that Abe Beame came out of, and they did know each other. Like all developers, my father and I contributed to Beame, and to other politicians. The simple fact is that contributing money to politicians is very standard and accepted for a New York City developer. We didn't give any more to Beame than a lot of other developers did. In fact, it often seemed to me that, perhaps because we knew Beame personally, he almost went out of his way to avoid any appearance that he was doing us any special favors.

"Instead I spent most of the four years when Beame was mayor trying to promote the West 34th Street site for a convention center. It was by far the best site on the merits, and we eventually got nearly big-name New York City businessmen behind us. Still, Beame never came out in support of the site until a few weeks before he left office. Nor did he give it his official approval. It was Ed Koch, newly elected in 1978, who finally chose our site for the convention center. No one, as far as I know, has ever suggested that Donald Trump and Ed Koch are close personal friends. But that's getting way ahead of the story."

With all the commotion about this young upstart hitting the city with huge tax credits and proposing a convention center, Trump began to get press without the benefit of planning his own announcements. The remarks that were said were sometimes rude and biting. At one point, according to Mr. Trump, someone told one of his friends that "Trump has a great line of shit, but where are the bricks and mortar?"

"I remember being outraged when I heard that, and I didn't speak to this guy for more than a year. But looking back, I can see he was right. It all could have gone up in smoke. If I hadn't managed to make one of those first projects happen, if I hadn't finally convinced the city to choose my West 34th Street site for its convention center and then gone on to develop the Grand Hyatt, I'd probably be back in Brooklyn today, collecting rents. I had a lot riding on those first projects.

"On July 29, 1974, we announced that the Trump Organization had secured options to purchase the two waterfront sites from the Penn Central—West 59th Street to West 72nd Street, and West 34th Street to West 39th Street—at a cost of $62 million. With no money down. The story made the front page of the New York *Times*.

"My original idea was to build middle-income housing on the sites at rents that seem ridiculously cheap today—$110 to $125 a room—but were considered moderately high at the time. I planned to seek financing from the Mitchel-Lama program, through which the city provided low-interest long-term mortgages and tax abatements to builders. The program had been initiated to encourage middle-income housing.''

February, 1975, was a bad year to try to build housing in New York. The Urban Development Corporation was the state agency that was to provide the housing financing for new middle-income housing, the very type that Trump had in mind to build. However, Mayor Beame announced that the Urban Development Corporation had defaulted on $100 million of repayment on its bonds. Later on that year, the state of New York announced that it was also temporarily suspending all of its housing financing, because of the well publicized fiscal crises. The possibilities of Donald Trump building through financing were very low, and he decided to try something else. Like a new convention center, which he pursued immediately.

Donald began hiring people to help with his new convention center proposal, which was to be built on his 34th Street site. He also set his sights on the ailing Commodore Hotel, after asking Victor Palmieri if he had access to any other properties with major investment potential. Palmieri offered the Commodore to Trump, and the rest is history. Mr. Trump liked the place right away. Hoards of people were walking past the run down place, getting off the subway, or as they walked to work. Mr. Trump sensed that the place could be suited to fit an affluent market once again, as it once did in the past.

His newly formed team of professionals included Roy Cohn, Louise Sunshine (an experienced financial consultant with many political connections), and public relations executive Howard Rubenstein. "But even as I was assembling a team to promote my site," Trump wrote, "the city and state were hatching their own alternative: to put the convention center in Battery Park City, opposite the World Trade Center in Southern Manhattan. In my opinion, both sites—West 44th Street and Battery Park—were terrible choices. Making my case was another matter. I wanted to wage battle in public, but I was an unknown. If I was going to attract attention for my site and win support for it, I had to raise my profile.

"I decided to call my first news conference. Louise and Howard Rubenstein, a major New York public relations executive, helped attract support from several people, including Manfred Ohrenstein, majority leader of the state senate, and Theodore Kheel, the labor negotiator, who was very powerful in New York politics. Kheel delivered a classic line at the press conference. 'Placing the new convention center in Battery Park,' he said, 'is like putting a nightclub in a graveyard.' For our part, we put up a huge banner that said, 'Miracle on 34th Street' and I announced, before a ton of reporters, that I could build my convention center for $110 million—or at least $150 million less than the city had estimated it would cost to build at West 44th Street.

"Not surprisingly, that raised some eyebrows and even got us some attention in the press. But there was scarcely an approving peep from the politicians. I discovered, for the first time but not for the last, that politicians don't care too much what things cost. It's not their money.

"In promoting my site, the first thing I pointed out wherever I went was how important it was to build a convention center. A lot of people were saying that the best solution, in light of the city's fiscal crisis, was to scrap the idea altogether.

"To me," Trump said, "that was classic short-sightedness. For example, in the face of a sales drop, most companies cut back on their advertising budgets. But in fact, you need advertising the most when people aren't buying. Essentially, that's what I said about a convention center. Building one, I argued, was critical to reviving the city's image and, ultimately, to putting its economy back on track.

"I also told anyone who would listen how great my site was, and how horrible the alternatives were. I pointed out that at 44th Street the convention center would have to be built on platforms over the water, which would be more costly, more problematic, and ultimately more time consuming. I said that the 44th Street site was too small, that there was no room to expand it, and that because it was on the water, you'd have to cross under the crumbling West Side Highway to get to it. Finally, I made a big deal out of the fact that you needed something called a nonnavigable permit to build on the 44th Street site. A nonnavigable permit, which I became an expert about very quickly, is the federal approval required to build on certain waterways, and getting it requires an act of congress.

"I was just as rough on the Battery Park site, which was an even more ridiculous location at the absolute southern tip of the city. I pointed out how remote it was from mid-town, how far from hotels and entertainment, and how inconvenient to public transportation. I also circulated a state study which concluded that building a convention center at Battery Park would require major reconstruction of the West Side Highway leading to it, as well as the addition of at least 2,000 new hotel rooms.

"Most of all, I talked about what a wonderful location I had on West 34th Street. It was on the right side of the highway—the eastern side—which meant it was easily accessible. It was closer to subways and buses than the alternative sites. I continued to make the case that the center could be built more cheaply on my site without dispossessing any tenants. Also, because my site was so big, there was plenty of room for expansion in the future. When a group of graduate students in a class taught by City Councilman Robert Wagner did a little study that rated our site the best, I managed to get hold of it and immediately christened it the Wagner Report. Its namesake wasn't thrilled.

"Before long, I had everything going for me except the support of a few absolutely key people. Abe Beame was at the top of the list. Once he gave up on West 44th Street, Beame got behind Battery Park, and no matter how many great arguments I came up with for my site, he wouldn't budge. Another major opponent was John Zuccotti, a deputy mayor under Beame. He began going around town bad-mouthing my site. The reason, I'm convinced, was that he didn't want to admit that he'd wasted several years of his life and millions of dollars of public money on a location that never made sense in the first place. And that's exactly what I said publicly. I accused him of being self-serving and petty and a half dozen other things. He got pretty riled up. The battle received a lot of media attention, and ultimately, I think, it was good for my site. It became just another way to promote my site's many advantages.

"In the end, we won by wearing everyone else down. We never gave up, and the opposition slowly began to melt away. In 1977 Beame appointed yet another committee to study the alternative sites, and it concluded that we did have the best site. On that basis, Beame finally gave us his support— although not his signature—just before leaving office at the end of the year.''

Ed Koch took over as mayor of New York and decided to go ahead and do his own study for the convention center sites, in 1978. In April of that year, the results were in, and the city announced that the 34th Street site was by far the very best location. The city and state announced that they would purchase Donald Trump's site, and build the long awaited convention center there. Although there was a lot of money in this deal for Donald Trump, there was also a fair amount of credibility given to him personally. Trump says that he actually lost money on the deal, but that the confidence the project instilled in him according to his many detractors, made the deal worthwhile.

"As my deal with the Penn Central was structured, I was paid total compensation of about $833,000 based on the $12 million price for the site that the city negotiated with Penn Central. In the end I offered to forgo my fee altogether, if the city would agree to name the convention center after my family. I've been criticized for trying to make that trade, but I have no apologies. There wouldn't be a new convention center in New York today if it hadn't been for the Trumps.

"More important," Trump insisted, "the city would have saved a fortune by letting me build the center, which I very much wanted to do. Instead, Ed Koch decided, by some logic I could never understand, that because I'd helped arrange the sale of the property, it was a conflict for me to be the builder as well. Eventually, I offered the city a deal that, frankly, was ridiculous for me. I said I would bring the entire job in for less than $200 million, and that if there were any overruns, I'd pay for them myself. You won't find many builders willing to put themselves on the line that way.

"Instead, the city and state decided to oversee the job—and the result was perhaps the most horrendous construction delays and cost overruns in the history of the building business. A man named Richard Kahan was put in charge of the Urban Development Corporation, and ultimately it was his job to oversee the convention center project. Richard Kahan is a nice man, but he had visions of being the next Robert Moses. It wasn't clear that he had the experience or the talent.

"One of the first things Kahan did was to hire I.M. Pei as his architect. I.M. Pei is a man with a terrific reputation, but in my view he often chooses the most expensive solution to a problem—and is virtually uncontrollable. Immediately, Pei decided to design a space frame for the center—a structural system that any professional builder will tell you is one of the most difficult to build and is especially vulnerable to cost overruns. This is particularly true when you're dealing with the sort of huge space frame they needed for a convention center.

"From the very start, I told Kahan and his people that it was critical to build a parking garage simultaneously. How can you have a convention center without parking? They told me that a garage would hold up the city's environmental-impact approval. 'Look,' I said to them, 'those approvals are only going to be tougher to get later, and at the very least you should begin a separate filing for the garage now, so you can at least start the process.' They ignored me, and now they have no parking, and no prospect of building any in the near future.

"The choice of where to put the entrance was equally ill-considered. If you put the entrance at the west, the whole center faces the Hudson River, which is a beautiful view. Instead, they built the entrance on the eastern side of the building—facing the traffic on Eleventh Avenue.

"As I watched these mistakes being made, I became very angry and frustrated. In 1983, when it was clear the construction of the convention center was already a disaster of delays and overruns, I wrote a letter to William Stern, who by then had replaced Richard Kahan as president of the Urban Development Corporation. For a second time I offered, this time for no fee at all, to oversee the project and to assure that it would get completed quickly and without further cost overruns.

"My offer was refused—and a disaster eventually turned into a catastrophe. By the time the convention center was finally finished last year, it was four years behind schedule—and at least $250 million over budget. When you add interest—the carrying costs for all those years of construction—the total cost was probably $1 billion, or $700 million over budget.

"The construction was a terrible disgrace, and all the worse because no one raised a fuss about it. When I was invited to attend opening day ceremonies in 1986, I refused. What happened at the convention center is that the city and state took a great piece of property and a great project and ruined it through terrible planning and ridiculous cost overruns. Even if the convention center is ultimately a success, it can never earn back all the money that was unnecessarily squandered to build it."

The acquisition and eventual renovation of the Commodore Hotel, bordering New York's prestigious Park Avenue and 42nd Street, has been one of the most talked about ventures during Donald Trump's excitingly short real estate career. This intense project took years of careful planning, sharp business instincts, and keen intuition. At the time of Mr. Trump's purchase of the building, it was considered a ramshackly eyesore, directly adjacent Grand Central Station.

Gary Belis of *Fortune* has said that "the renovation of the old Commodore Hotel at the height of New York's fiscal crises [was], a considerable accomplishment that sparked the revival of East 42nd Street." The success story of the complicated revamping of the Commodore Hotel into the bold exciting look of the new Grand Hyatt, is a tale of endurance and spirited belief in a prosperous future.

"Flair." That's how Donald Trump was credited, in the New York *Times,* during his 1976 entreprenurial designs. In an almost gushing article, Judy Klemesrud wrote of Trump's dealings with the Commodore Hotel, the proposed convention center, and the two large railyards of Manhattan's west side.

"He is tall, lean, and blond, with dazzling white teeth, and he looks ever so much like Robert Redford," began Ms. Klemesrud's piece. "He rides around town in a chauffeured silver Cadillac with his initials, DJT, on the plates.

"Flair. It's one of Donald Trump's favorite words, and both he, his friends, and his enemies use it when describing his way of life as well as his business style as New York's No. 1 real estate promoter of the middle 1970's.

" 'If a man has flair,' the energetic, outspoken Mr. Trump said the other day, 'and is smart and somewhat conservative and has a taste for what people want, he's bound to be successful in New York.'

"Mr. Trump, who is president of the Brooklyn-based Trump Organization which owns and manages 22,000 apartments, currently has three imaginative projects in the works. And much to his delight, his brash, controversial style has prompted comparisons with his flamboyant idol, the late William Zeckendorf, Sr., who actually developed projects as striking as those Mr. Trump is proposing.

"The proposed projects are:

• A large Manhattan convention center over the Penn Central Transportation Company's 34th Street yards. Mr. Trump, who acquired the development rights from the bankrupt railroad, has drawn up plans for a $90 million center, hoping it will replace the stalled convention center on the Hudson River from 43rd to 47th Street.

• A 1,500-room Hyatt Regency hotel following the reconstruction of Penn Central's Commodore Hotel near Grand Central Terminal. Last April, Mr. Trump received a controversial $4 million a year tax abatement from the city, the first of its kind, for his proposal to rebuild the aging hotel building.

• Construction of 14,500 federally subsidized apartments on the Penn Central's 60th Street yards, to which Mr. Trump has acquired the development rights. The site is bounded by West 59th and West 72nd Street, West End Avenue and the Hudson River.

" 'What makes Donald Trump so significant right now,' said one Manhattan real estate expert, 'is that there is nobody else who is a private promoter on a major scale, trying to convince entrepreneurs to develop major pieces of property.'

"Commenting on the Commodore Hotel, the expert said he thought Mr. Trump was 'on the threshold of the greatest real estate coup of the last miserable three years.'

"The other day, Mr. Trump, who says he is publicity shy, allowed a reporter to accompany him on what he described as a typical work day. It consisted mainly of visits to his 'jobs,' the term he uses for housing projects owned by the Trump Organization, which was founded by his 70-year old father, Fred C. Trump, now the company's chairman.

"The day began at 7:45 A.M. when Mr. Trump's chauffeur, Robert Utsey, a husky, gun toting laid-off New York City policeman who doubles as a bodyguard, pulled the Cadillac up in front of the Phoenix apartment building, at 160 East Street."

Ms. Klemesrud described Mr. Trump's appearance in the mid-seventies, a look that he has shed, in favor of the sharp, clean, dynamic look that he shows today. "Mr. Trump, who lives in a three bedroom apartment done mostly in beiges and browns and lots of chrome, was waiting in front of the building. He is 6 feet 3 inches tall and weighs 190 pounds, and he was wearing a three-piece burgundy wool suit, matching patent leather shoes, and a white shirt with the initials 'DJT' sewn in burgundy thread on the cuffs.

"Speaking occasionally on his car telephone to his secretary and his banker at Chase Manhattan, Mr. Trump directed his chauffeur to make stops at the 60th Street yards; the convention center site; a federally subsidized Trump housing project for the aged in East Orange, N.J., which he calls 'our philanthropic endeavor'; a middle-income housing project on Staten Island; the flagship 4,000-unit Trump Village in Brooklyn and several other older Trump-owned projects in Brooklyn that the company bought in recent years.

" 'That's one of the reasons for our success— while others were building over the last three or four years at 10 percent interest, we were buying, at 5 ½ percent mortgages,' Mr. Trump said. 'And the units they produced in their new buildings were much smaller than the ones we were buying.' "

Ms. Klemesrud also showed the developing businessman at a very strong point in his life. He had the nervous aggression of youth, while watching his own business acumin hone to a hard professional edge. "Although the Trumps have been building in New York City since 1923, the family has not gotten as much publicity as other real estate developers because they didn't enter the Manhattan market until three years ago.

" 'It was psychology,' Mr. Trump explained. 'My father knew Brooklyn very well, and he knew

Queens very well. But now, that psychology has ended.'

"One of the reasons for the current intense push in Manhattan," Klemesrud wrote, "is that the Trump organization, with 15,000 of its 22,000 apartments situated in New York City (mostly in Brooklyn, Queens, and Staten Island), has a stake in the future of the city.

"The organization, which is made up of 60 partnerships and corporations, also owns apartment buildings in Washington, D.C., Maryland, and Virginia and land in California and Las Vegas, and it employs about 1,000 people.

" 'New York is either going to get much better or much worse,' Mr. Trump predicted, 'and I think it will get much better. I'm not talking about the South Bronx. I don't know anything about the South Bronx.

" 'But in Manhattan, I feel a new convention center will be a turning point for the city. It will get rid of all that pornographic garbage in Times Square. Psychologically, I think, if New York City gets a convention center, it will resurge and rejuvenate.'

"As he drove around the city, he exclaimed boyishly, 'Look at that great building (at 56th Street and Madison Avenue). It's available! There are a lot of good deals around right now.'

"What attracts him to the real estate business? 'I love the architectural creativeness,' he said. 'For example, the Commodore Hotel is one of the most important locations in the city, and its reconstruction will lead to a rebirth of that area.

" 'And I like the financial creativeness, too. There's a beauty in putting together a financial package that really works, whether it be through tax credits, or a mortgage financing arrangement, or a leaseback arrangement.

" 'Of course, the gamble is an exciting part, too,' he said grinning. 'No matter how much you take out of it, you're talking about $100 million deals, where a 10 percent mistake is $10 million. But so far, I've never made a bad deal.'

"Donald Trump was in the headlines in 1973," Klemesrud wrote in her 1976 article, "when the Department of Justice brought suit against the Trump Organization, charging discrimination against blacks in apartment rentals. Mr. Trump denied the charges, and later signed an agreement to provide open-housing opportunities for minority groups.

" 'We never discriminated against blacks," Mr. Trump said angrily. " 'Five to 10 percent of our units are rented to blacks in the city. But we won't sign leases with welfare clients unless they have gauranteed income levels, because otherwise everyone immediately starts leaving the building.' "

It was during this time, that Donald Trump met his lawyer and long time advisor, Roy M. Cohn. Much has been written about the late Cohn since his AIDS related death. A biography is on the stands, detailing the events of Cohn's life, and parts of his story are incredible. Donald Trump wrote about his dealings with Cohn and some personal opinions. At the time of their initial meeting, Mr. Trump had been frequenting the exclusive clubs in Manhattan, and he happened to meet Cohn at one of them.

"It was at Le Club that I first met Roy Cohn. I knew him by reputation and was aware of his image as a guy who wasn't afraid to fight. One night I found myself sitting at the table next to him. We got introduced, and we talked for a while, and I challenged him. I like to test people. I said to him, 'I don't like lawyers. I think all they do is delay deals, instead of making deals, and every answer they give you is no, and they are always looking to settle instead of fight.' He said he agreed with me. I liked that and so then I said, 'I'm just not built that way. I'd rather fight than fold, because as soon as you fold once, you get the reputation of being a folder.'

"I could see Roy was intrigued," Trump said, "but he wasn't sure what the point of it all was. Finally he said, 'Is this just an academic conversation?'

"I said, 'No, it's not academic at all. It just happens that the government has just filed suit against our company and many others, under the civil rights act, saying that we discriminated against blacks in some of our housing developments.' I explained to him that I'd spent that afternoon with my father, talking to lawyers in a very prestigious Wall Street firm, and they'd advised us to settle. That's exactly what most businessmen do when the government charges them with anything, because they just don't want bad publicity, even if they believe they can beat a phony rap.

"The idea of settling drove me crazy. The fact was that we did rent to blacks in our buildings. What we didn't do was rent to welfare cases, white or black. I'd watched what happened when the government came after Samuel Lefrak, another builder, and he caved in and started taking welfare cases. They virtually ruined his buildings.

"We wanted tenants who we could be sure would pay the rent, who would be neat and clean and good neighbors, and who met our requirement of having an income of at least four times the rent. So he said, 'My view is tell them to go to hell and fight the thing in court and let them prove that you discriminated, which seems to me very difficult to do, in view of the fact that you have black tenants in the building.' He also told me, "I don't think you have any obligation to rent to tenants who would be undesirable, white or black, and the government doesn't have a right to ruin your business.' "

"That's when I decided Roy Cohn was the right person to handle the case. I was nobody at the time, but he loved a good fight, and he took my case. He went to court, and I went with him, and we fought the charges. In the end the government couldn't prove its case, and we ended up making a minor settlement without admitting any guilt. Instead, we agreed to do some equal-opportunity advertising of vacancies for a period of time in the local newspaper. And that was the end of the suit.

"I learned a lot about Roy during that period. He was a great lawyer when he wanted to be. He could go into a case without any notes. He had a photographic memory and could argue the facts from his head. When he was prepared, he was brilliant and almost unbeatable. However, he wasn't always prepared. Even then, he was so brilliant that he could sometimes get away with it. Unfortunately, he could also be a disaster, and so I would always question Roy very closely before a court date. If he wasn't prepared, I'd push for a postponement.

"I don't kid myself about Roy. He was no Boy Scout. He once told me that he'd spent more than two-thirds of his adult life under indictment on one charge or another. That amazed me. I said to him, 'Roy, just tell me one thing. Did you really do all that stuff?' He looked at me and smiled. 'What the hell do you think?' he said. I never really knew.

"Whatever else you could say about Roy, he was very tough. Sometimes I think that next to loyalty, toughness was the most important thing in the world to him. For example, all Roy's friends knew he was gay, and if you saw him socially, he was invariably with some very good looking young man. But Roy never talked about it. He just didn't like the image. He felt that to the average person, being gay was almost synonymous with being a wimp. That was the last thing he wanted to project, so he almost went overboard to avoid it. If the subject of gay rights came up, Roy was always the first to speak out against them.

"Tough as he was, Roy always had a lot of friends, and I'm not embarrassed to say I was one," Trump admitted. "He was a truly loyal guy—it was a matter of honor with him—and because he was also very smart, he was a great guy to have on your side. You could count on him to go to bat for you, even if he privately disagreed with your view, and even if defending you wasn't necessarily the best thing for him. He was never two-faced.

"Just compare that with all the hundreds of 'respectable' guys who make careers out of boasting about their uncompromising integrity but have absolutely no loyalty. They think only about what is best for them and don't think twice about stabbing a friend in the back if the friend becomes a problem. What I liked best about Roy Cohn was that he would do just the opposite. Roy was the sort of guy who'd be there at your hospital bed, long after everyone else had bailed out, literally standing by you to the death.''

Roy Cohn represented Mr. Trump in many a courtroom battle, after their initial efforts with the discrimination suits. One of the more important of these was a battle to build the Trump Tower. Many legal obstacles were in the way, and Donald Trump needed as competent a lawyer as he could find. It turned out that Cohn was the man for the job. ''We won in Supreme Court,'' Mr. Trump wrote of being turned down for an application for a large tax incentive offered by New York City, ''got overturned at the appellate level, and ended up again before the court of appeals. My lawyer, Roy Cohn, did a brilliant job, arguing before seven justices without so much as a note. This time, the court again ruled unanimously that we were entitled to our exemption—and ordered the city to provide it without further delay.''

''Fellow real estate executives in the very close knit industry also say mostly nice things about Donald Trump,'' Judy Klemesrud wrote, ''even when given the chance to speak off the record.

'' 'He's a very adventurous young man, and we're all rooting for him,' said Samuel J. Lefrak, of the Lefrak Organization. 'He's bold, soaring, and swashbuckling. But in my opinion, the jury is still out.'

''Harry B. Helmsley of Helmsley-Spear, Inc., said that although he had never had any dealings with Mr. Trump, he found him to be 'very active around town. I just hope he can put his deals together.'

"Even Preston Robert Tisch, president of Loews Corporation, who is regarded as Mr. Trump's No. 1 critic in the city, spoke highly of the young promoter. 'He's a very bright, capable real estate man.'

"Real estate insiders say Mr. Tisch and Mr. Trump are at odds for two reasons—the Commodore Hotel tax abatement deal (Mr. Tisch's company owns the hotels), and the 34th Street convention center site (Mr. Tisch was long associated with the rival 44th Street convention center site).

"Criticism of Mr. Trump came mainly from mortgage bankers and others in the money end of the real estate industry, all of whom requested anonymity.

" 'His deals are dramatic, but they haven't come into being,' said one. 'So far, the chief beneficiary of his creativity has been his public image.'

"Another money man called Mr. Trump 'overrated' and 'totally obnoxious,' and said much of his influence has to do with the fact that he was an early financial supporter of both Governor Carey and Mayor Beame and had a powerful lawyer (Roy M. Cohn) and a powerful public relations man (Howard Rubinstein).

"Mr. Trump has been meeting the right people. During lunch at the 21 Club, the waiters were bowing and saying, 'Hello Donald,' and other lunchers, including Mr. Helmsley and assorted politicians, stopped by to say hello.

"Mr. Trump took exactly one hour for lunch, during which he ate broiled filet of sole, with no butter, drank ginger ale, and chatted with two men representing the National Jewish Hospital in Denver, which plans to name him their Man of the Year on December 8 at a dinner in the Waldorf Astoria Hotel.

" 'I'm not even Jewish, I'm Swedish,' he said later. 'Most people think my family is Jewish because we own so many buildings in Brooklyn. But I guess you don't have to be Jewish to win this award, because they told me a gentile won it one other year.'

"Mr. Trump spent a profitable afternoon earning a $140,000 commission for about 20 minutes work selling part of a housing project for a friend. A witness to the negotiations said Mr. Trump was a hard-nosed broker, refusing to budge from his original terms of $1.4 million paid over a four-year period at 9 percent interest.

"The transaction took place at the architectural offices of Poor, Swanke, Hayden & Connell, at 400 Park Avenue, where Mr. Trump had gone to visit Der Scutt, the architect of his proposed $90 million convention center.

" 'Donald's very demanding,' the pipe smoking Mr. Scutt said when the promoter was out of the room.

"When I asked whether he thought Mr. Trump had any shortcomings, the architect replied; 'He's extremely aggressive when he sells, maybe to the point of overselling. Like, he'll say the convention center is the biggest in the world, when it really isn't. He'll exaggerate for the purpose of making a sale.'

"Mr. Trump ended his 'typical day' by catching a plane to California, where he said he planned to wrap up a 'multi-million dollar' land deal. He has been spending more and more of his time in the Los Angeles area lately, staying in a house that he owns, complete with swimming pool and tennis court, in Beverly Hills.

"Is there any danger that Donald Trump will defect to the West Coast? 'Some of the best deals I've made have been land deals in California,' he said with a smile. 'I've probably made $14 million there over the last two years. But my friends and enemies are in New York, so I'll probably stay here.' "

Much has changed since Donald Trump spent the day with Judy Klemesrud. The Commodore is now the Grand Hyatt, the convention center is built (however poorly), and Donald's reputation as a builder, as well as a deal maker, has grown considerably. In 1980, only one month until the Grand Hyatt had its official reopening, Howard Blum wrote a lengthy article on Donald Trump, and his accomplishments of the time. "More than any developer of his generation, 34 year old Donald J. Trump has succeeded over the last decade in reshaping the skyline of Manhattan. Taking advantage of political connections, a large family fortune, and a salesman's aggressive optimism, he has effectively influenced the changing character of mid-town.

"He is responsible for the 1,407-room Grand Hyatt Hotel on East 42nd Street, the 56-story Trump Tower going up at the site of the old Bonwit Teller building on Fifth Avenue and 57th Street, and the current development of the block between 61st and 62nd Streets on Third Avenue. And he was the catalyst behind the state's decision to build a convention center at 34th Street.

"But recently Mr. Trump has received more attention for what he has destroyed than what he has built. As the work progressed on Trump Tower, which is scheduled for completion by 1982, he ordered the demolition of an intricate and architecturally important Art Deco frieze that had decorated the building he was tearing down.

"The destruction of the artwork not-withstanding, Mr. Trump's success in making the Trump Tower a reality is the culmination of the nearly two decades he has spent trying to realize his ambitions in real estate—ambitions that had their roots, he says now, in an experience 16 years ago.

"On a November afternoon in 1964, in a cold, relentless rain, 18-year-old Donald Trump attended the ceremonies for the opening of the Verrazano Narrows Bridge. There, standing in the midst of this foul weather, he had a sudden realization, an epiphany that, he says now, always remained with him, shaping the way he made his fortune in real estate in New York City.

" 'The rain was coming down for hours while all these jerks were being introduced and praised,' recalled Mr. Trump, who had gone to the festivities as a college freshman with his father, a real estate developer. 'But all I'm thinking about is that all these politicians who opposed the bridge are being applauded. Yet, in a corner, just standing there in the rain is this man, this 85-year-old engineer who came from Sweden and designed this bridge, who poured his heart into it, and nobody even mentioned his name.

" 'I realized then and there,' Mr. Trump concluded, 'that if you let people treat you how they want, you'll be made a fool. I realized then and there something I would never forget. I don't want to be made anybody's sucker.'

"Turning 30 in 1976, Mr. Trump found himself ready to climb up the ladder of social visibility by bringing his deals out of the boroughs where his father had made a substantial fortune, and into Manhattan. While the father had appeared for years at Brooklyn political dinners, the son would purchase tables for ballet galas. Now, as the younger Mr. Trump saw it, the empire of approximately

22,000 rental units spreading profitably throughout Queens and Brooklyn would provide a base on which to build.

"The strength of Mr. Trump's New York political connections is reflected in the simple fact that in Governor Carey's last campaign, only Mr. Carey's brother contributed more than the Trump's $135,000.

"Deputy Mayor Robert F. Wagner, Jr., who as the former head of the City Planning Commission has had many dealings with Mr. Trump, said, 'It wasn't political connections that made Donald Trump successful. He tends to exaggerate a bit, but it's a salesman's exaggeration. And Donald could be very convincing when he's selling a project to the city.'

"For his part, Mr. Trump said that 'by having me directly involved in the project it becomes 25 percent more valuable.' "

Mr. Blum then stepped into one of the more touchy areas of Donald Trump's business persona. " 'After the decision was made to build the convention center on the 34th Street site, we met with Trump because he had been awarded the option on the property after Penn Central went into bankruptcy,' said Peter J. Solomon, former Deputy Mayor for Economic Development.

" 'Trump told us he was entitled to a $4.4 million commission on the sale according to his contract with Penn Central. But he told us he'd forgo his fee if we would name the convention center after his father—the Fred C. Trump Convention Center.

" 'We thought about it and we came to the conclusion that it might be worth the $4.4 million. But, after a month of knocking the idea around, someone finally read the terms of the original Penn Central contract with Trump. He wasn't entitled to anywhere near the money he was claiming. Based on the sales price we had negotiated, his fee was only about $500,000.

" 'But what really got me," Mr. Solomon continued, 'was his bravado. It was fantastic. It was unbelievable. He almost got us to name the convention center after his father in return for something he never really had to give away. I guess he just thought we would never read the fine print or by the time we did, the deal to name the building after his father would have been set.'

"Mr. Trump said he received a $500,000 commission and $88,000 in expenses for the sale of the 34th Street site to the Urban Development Corporation and, not denying Mr. Solomon's version of events, added that if the site had been sold for more than $14 million he would have been entitled to a larger, escalating commission.

" 'If someone came to me properly,' he insisted, 'I would have given up my commission without asking that they put my father's name on the building. But they didn't.'

"Asked why he wanted his father's name on the convention center, Mr. Trump said, 'Let's just say my family would deserve an honor like that. If it was not for me, there would be no convention center in this city.'

"City Councilman Henry J. Stern agreed that Donald Trump played a significant role in persuading the Governor to select the 34th Street location over two other sites.

" 'Donald Trump runs with the same clique that continues to manipulate things behind the scenes in this city,' Mr. Stern said. 'He has access through his father to the Brooklyn Democratic machine that produced Hugh Carey. Roy Cohn is his lawyer. He throws around a lot of money in political campaigns!'

"Mr. Trump's political connections, according to Mr. Stern, enable him to negotiate a 'sweetheart contract' with the Metropolitan Transportation Authority for the purpose of a tennis club in Grand Central Terminal. The authority, in giving Mr. Trump the 20-year lease, rejected a significantly higher bid.

" 'The M.T.A. wanted someone who could make a big investment to repair and maintain those courts,' Mr. Trump said. 'By giving me the contract, they knew they had someone who had the assets to do just that. It was in no political favor.'

"Roy M. Cohn, who describes himself as 'not only Donald's lawyer, but also one of his close friends,' said, 'Donald wishes he didn't have to give money to politicians, but he knows it's part of the game. He doesn't try to get anything for it; he's just doing what a lot of people in the real estate business try to do.'

"Perhaps Mr. Trump's most politically influenced deal," Mr. Blum wrote, "was his buying the Commodore Hotel from the bankrupt Penn Central Corporation for $10 million and then selling the hotel to the Urban Development Corporation for $1. Mr. Trump and members of his family—along with his 50 percent partners in the project—would run the hotel for 99 years, while the city received income dependent upon the hotel's profitability. The hotel would be renovated by Mr. Trump and his partner, the Hyatt Corporation, and run as the Grand Hyatt Hotel. At the end of the 99-year leasehold, the property would revert to the city.

"But, in the most controversial aspect of the deal, the Grand Hyatt Hotel received 40 years of tax abatements that would be worth about $56 million to Mr. Trump and his partners.

" 'Clearly the city could have gotten a better deal,' said Deputy Mayor Wagner, who criticized the tax abatements as a City Councilman. 'But Donald Trump made his deal at a time when the city was desperate for development. Also, he had the vision to have picked the Commodore site when he did. You've got to remember when Trump bought the Commodore, East 42nd Street was going downhill, and nobody was building hotels in New York.

" 'Now, it seems developers like Trump helped turn all that around, even if they got away with a bit too much in the process.'

"The Hyatt Hotel is expected to open this fall. Architecturally, what Mr. Trump calls the hotel's 'sleek glass frame' has already been criticized. 'It is the sort of flashy hotel one would find in Atlanta or Houston, but certainly not in New York,' wrote Paul Goldberger in the New York *Times*. 'It is essentially an out-of-towner's vision of city life.' "

Mr. Blum went on to say that, "Mr. Trump has not achieved the type of public spirited recognition he and his public-relations people have been seeking. Rather, his destruction of the Bonwit's frieze last June—motivated in large part by the desire to save $500,000 on a $100 million project—brought him publicity of a less welcome sort.

"His boldly comfortable style of living is supported by a considerable personal fortune. People in the real estate business estimate the worth of the Trump Organization properties at approximately $200 million," Blum wrote in 1980. "Mr. Trump's personal banker, Conrad Stevenson of Chase, said, 'Donald Trump was a wealthy man when he was born, and he's more wealthy now.' "

" 'My biggest concern,' Donald Trump said of the need to destroy certain existing elements, 'was

the safety of the people on the street below.'
There was a public outcry when it was announced
that Trump would be forced to tear down the
building's 'treasures.'

"The workers demolishing the Fifth Avenue store
destroyed two Art Deco bas-relief sculptures and a
grillwork of intricate geometric design. Several
months earlier, Mr. Trump had pledged the pieces
to the Metropolitan Museum of Art, provided the
cost and technical problems of removing them were
not prohibitive.

" 'If one of those stones had slipped, people
could have been killed,' Mr. Trump responded.

"He also said his decision had been influenced
by the potential cost of the removal of the artwork—
more than $500,000, he said, in taxes, interest, and
rental loss caused by delays in construction.

" 'There is nothing I would like to do more
than give something to a museum,' he said in a
recent interview.

" 'Why?'

" 'I've always been interested in art,' Mr. Trump
told them.

"A visitor observed that there was no art in Mr.
Trump's office.

"The developer considered this for a moment.
Then, with a smile, he pointed to an idealized
illustration of Trump Tower hanging on the walls.

" 'If that isn't art,' Mr. Trump said, 'then I
don't know what is.' "

"In 1975," James R. Norman said in *Business Week,* "when he was 28 years old, he proposed an ambitious scheme to remake the aging Commodore Hotel above Grand Central Station into the luxury Grand Hyatt, aided by hefty tax breaks. With New York on the brink of bankruptcy, it was a courageous proposal—and one the city warmly embraced. Since then he has ridden New York's real estate boom to impressive heights, erecting his luxury condo projects at a rate of about one a year.

"Trump has always courted publicity and controversy, often with an eye for the grand gesture. In the 1970s he offered to build what is now the Jacob Javits Convention Center in New York for $170 million if the city would name the building after his father. The city declined."

The best personal listings publication, *Current Biography*, wrote about the Commodore/Hyatt deal. "When Donald Trump proposed in 1976 to buy the Commodore with the intention of renovating it, the hotel had been losing some $1.5 million a year and had not paid any taxes to the city for several years. Fred Trump disapproved of the purchase, saying, 'This is like trying to buy a ticket on the Titanic.' But Donald Trump, unperturbed by the Commodore's losses and the poor condition of the city's then finances, worked out a fifty-fifty joint venture with the Hyatt Corporation and then proceeded to negotiate a forty-year tax abatement from the city—the first of its kind ever granted to a commercial property. Hotel expert Bjorn Hanson of the accounting firm of Laventhal & Horwath estimated the value of the tax break at about $45 million. 'Clearly the city could have gotten a better deal,' Deputy Mayor Robert Wagner, Jr., has said. 'But Donald Trump made his deal at a time when the city was desperate for development. Also, he had the vision to have picked the Commodore site when he did. You've got to remember, when Trump bought the Commodore, East 42nd Street was going downhill, and nobody was building hotels in New York.' ''

''Mr. Trump,'' wrote Randall Smith in the *Wall Street Journal*, ''is a real estate promoter, a kind of go-between, who matches would-be buyers with would-be sellers, arranges financing and paves the administrative way for big projects—and in the process gains an ownership stake himself.

''Mr. Trump takes it all one step further. Combining a huckster's flair for hyperbole with a shrewd business and political sense, he sells himself as well. He is driven in a fancy limousine and frequents trendy mid-town restaurants and clubs, weaving an aura of glamour and chic around his name, which he hopes will translate into prestige for his endeavors and profits for him.''

''In the process he has,'' says Richard Rosan, the president of the Real Estate Board of New York, ''attracted more public attention here at an early age than any other real estate developer since William Zeckendorf, Sr., the late developer who amassed a giant real estate empire in the late 1950s."

Mr. Trump's detractors criticize his fast talking and promotional style. "That's been the talent of all the great promoters, to have big, exciting projects identified with their name and other people's money," says Julien Studley, a Manhattan real estate broker. Scoffs another, "He got lucky."

Among his other attributes, Mr. Smith mentioned Donald Trump's Commodore/Hyatt deal, saying that it was a "$100 million luxury hotel he built with Hyatt Corp.," which "opened in 1980." Mr. Smith also mentioned the rather large tax incentives that seems to occupy any talk about Trump, that Donald received for the Commodore's renovation.

"Such tax abatements were, at that time, rare, and other hotel owners opposed them, because of the advantage the cost savings would give a new competitor. Some politicians branded the abatement a 'giveaway' but fears were running high. The city was in the midst of a fiscal crises, and the area around the hotel was shaky."

" 'There were signs the whole area was going down," says Stanley Friedman, then a deputy to Mayor Beame. Mr. Trump played on those fears, threatening to pull out of the project if he didn't win an acceptable abatement. He ultimately negotiated a 40-year tax break. Mr. Trump declines to estimate the current value of the tax break, but hotel expert Bjorn Hanson of the accounting firm of Laventhal & Horwath figures it at about $45 million. It is one of the biggest such abatements negotiated in New York.

In an attempt to enlighten people about some of the finer elements in Trump's deals, *Boardroom Reports* listed what they believe are the secrets of his success, in an article called, "What his book doesn't tell."

One of the major points the article showed, was titled "Terrific Timing." "Even people who don't like Donald Trump," the report stated, "have to admit that his first big deal—picking up the run-down Commodore Hotel near Grand Central Station in New York for a song and then turning it into the glitzy new Hyatt Regency—showed a masterful sense of timing. Other hotels were closing down all over New York, but Trump guessed right that there soon would be a market for modern luxury facilities."

The *Boardroom Report* began by saying, "Though he's best known for having a world-class ego and a great talent for garnering personal publicity, Donald Trump also has a masterful way of making big real estate deals and building things. We didn't find the true secrets of his success in his book—so *Boardroom* interviewed several of the country's top real estate magnates for you."

Some of the other "secrets" of Donald Trump,

according to the *Boardroom Report*, are the following: "Spreading risk. Unlike his wealthy father who never borrowed a dime for his construction projects in Brooklyn and Queens, Donald is very, very adept at persuading others to participate financially in his ambitious deals. Aim: To minimize his personal risk without losing control of the project.

"Example: Trump recently negotiated the purchase of two foundering condominiums in West Palm Beach for such a good price and with such favorable financing from the Bank of New York that even though the redecorated and renamed towers are still only about 30% sold, Trump himself will come out whole.

"Right now," the article continued, "he's stalled on a huge West Side redevelopment project that most real estate insiders feel is ill-conceived. As one realtor points out, however, Trump is very determined once he sets his goals. When necessary, he rethinks the project—and moves ahead in a different way to make sure it gets off the ground.

"Trump proved he was a get-the-job-done-right champ when he managed to complete the reconstruction of Central Park's Wollman skating rink well under budget—well ahead of schedule. In doing so, he bailed out the city, which had wasted tens of millions of dollars and many years doing the job wrong.

"Not everyone approves of his taste in design

and architecture, but all agree that Trump knows how to build a quality building.

"Trump's great strength: An exquisite sense of what the market wants, especially wealthy foreigners. They appreciate the value of Trump's use of top quality materials and his interesting design statements. Result: They're willing to pay more for the cachet of living in a Trump building. Besides, explains one real estate tycoon, the kind of taste that architects and urban planners like often doesn't sell.

"Example: The whole concept of below-ground retail space in such buildings as the General Motors Building. Though popular with artistic purists, such space is very difficult to rent because people don't like to shop below ground.

"Promotional Genius. His private demeanor is very different from the strident public persona that has him calling New York City Mayor Ed Koch a moron. Many business people who project a likable image are real devils to do deals with. With Trump, it's just the opposite. Instead of the aggressive, contentious braggart you see on talk shows, he's really very reasonable, charming, factual, courteous, and respectful.

"The consensus: Trump's genius for self-promotion is one of the secrets of his success. It encourages people to bring him deals and helps raise money to finance his projects. The flip side, however, is that the strident publicity turns others away. As one wise Manhattan real estate veteran observed, many wealthy people pride themselves on living in buildings that just have simple street numbers.

"Others point out that Trump's own descriptions of his deals are usually at least a bit exaggerated. When he implies that he's managed to buy a building that no one else knew was on the market, don't believe it, says one real estate promoter, noting that sellers are seldom naive. If Trump really wants a property he has to pay more for it to get it. But competitors concede that Trump has a vision that others lack.

"Trump's vision reached new heights of grandeur when he acquired 72% of the class B voting stock of Resorts International last summer for about $80 million—$135 a share. Later he made a tender offer for more voting stock at the same price. Then he made a tender offer for the company's non-voting class A stock at $15 a share—a brilliant move that would have given him shares that hold equal rights to the company's assets for a fraction of what he purchased the original shares for. (He ultimately withdrew the offer when it failed to win the Resorts board's approval. But the door was left open to better offers.)"

When it was suggested to Mr. Trump to refurbish the Commodore in its original design, he refused. He believed that to create a new and successful operation, an entirely new design would be needed. "In my view," he said, "staying with that look would have been suicide. I said to these critics, 'Hey, fellas, do me a favor and don't tell me about these great monuments, because the Chrysler Building is in foreclosure, the neighborhood is a disaster, and it's obvious something's not working. If you think I'm going to leave the facade of the old Commodore the way it is, you're crazy. There's no way.'

"It's strange how things can turn around. Many of the same critics and preservationists who hated the original concept of my building now love it. What they discovered is that by choosing this highly reflective glass, I've created four walls of mirrors. Now when you go across 42nd Street or go over the Park Avenue ramp and look up at the Grand Hyatt, you see the reflection of Grand Central Terminal, you might not have noticed at all.

"The other new element that had a dramatic effect was the lobby. Most hotels in New York are dull and unexciting. I was determined to make ours an event, a place people wanted to visit. We chose a luxurious brown paradiso marble for the floors. We used beautiful brass for the railings and columns. We built a 170-foot glass-enclosed restaurant pitched out over 42nd Street, which no one had ever done before. I'm convinced that if I'd left the Commodore the way it was—old and dull and nondescript—it would have had absolutely no impact, and it wouldn't be doing the business it is today."

Chapter 3
Donald's Wife, Ivana.

"We met at the Montreal Summer Olympics in August 1976. I'd dated a lot of other women by then, but I'd never gotten seriously involved with any of them. Ivana wasn't someone you dated casually. Ten months later, in April 1977, we were married."

—Donald J. Trump—

It is a well known fact that Donald Trump works very hard to acquire the best that is available to him, and once he puts his name on something, he works even harder to see that it remains the best, as it progressively gets better. In 1977, the Trump name found its way into that of Ivana Winkelmayr.

The two were introduced at a reception for Olympic athletes, at the Montreal Summer Olympics in 1976, and according to available sources, they both fell in love with each other almost immediately. Donald Trump had been carefully dating some of the lovely women found in Manhattan's exclusively posh nightclubs, with the quiet hope that one of them might be a suitable partner. With all his looking, Mr. Trump couldn't seem to find the right woman worth marrying, until he met Ivana.

Donald Trump has said that, "Ivana wasn't someone you dated casually," and after a few dates with the blonde beauty, he put aside his casual female interests, and pursued the tall model who had captured his heart in Montreal.

Mr. Trump realized that good things sometimes take a little time to fall into place, even a business deal cannot be established overnight, and a good personal relationship cannot be built in a night or two on the town.

Although Ivana and Donald did spend many a night and day out together at sporting events, at exclusive night spots, and the theatre, they both took the vital time it takes to grow together. Donald Trump enjoyed sharing the best that his world had to offer with Ivana, and Ivana shared some insight with Donald about the pleasures of having a solid, and compatible personal companion.

Early on in 1976, Judy Klemesrud spoke of Mr. Trump's bachelor status, saying that, "Mr. Trump is single, with no plans of getting married in the near future, although he said he was seeing one woman—a fashion model—fairly regularly. 'If I met the right woman, I might get married,' he said. 'But right now, I have everything I want or need.' ''

Donald Trump told Ms. Klemesrud that he liked to, "relax at night by taking a date to such clubs as El Morocco, Regine's, Le Club, or Doubles, or attending Knicks or Rangers games in Madison Square Garden." Then and now, Mr. Trump enjoys going to sporting events, and cannot help but be interested to the point of actually getting involved personally, such as his dealings with the Generals, boxing events such as the recent Larry Holmes and Mike Tyson bout in Atlantic City, and his interest in keeping the New England Patriots in New England. Mr. Trump likes to involve Ivana in his sporting interests also, as she shares the sporting enthusiasm that is so much a part of Donald Trump.

Robert Boyle wrote about Ivana in *Sports Illustrated*, during Donald's New Jersey Generals' short lived USFL days. "Affable and boyishly handsome Trump, and his blonde wife, Ivana, a Vienna-born competitive skier and model who gave birth to their third child on January 6, have recently been the golden couple of newspaper style pages. They dine at goatskin tables in their own Manhattan condo overlooking Central Park, wear designer clothes and ski in Aspen, Gstaad, and St. Moritz when not weekending at their Greenwich, Conn., estate.

'' 'Donald's brilliant,' says Ivana, an executive vice president in charge of interior design for the family owned Trump Organization. 'As a lot of people say, whatever he touches turns to gold.' Trump skis and plays an occasional game of golf or tennis, but he has no deep interests aside from his family, real estate, and the Generals.

"Trump met Ivana in 1976 at a party in Montreal. Born Ivana Winkelmayr to an Austrian mother and a Czech father, she was raised in Vienna and moved to Czechoslovakia at the age of 14 when her father, an architect, had the opportunity to design sports complexes. In Vienna, Ivana had become a promising swimmer, but in Czechoslovakia she gave up swimming to concentrate on skiing. She received her bachelor's and master's degrees in physical education from Charles University in Prague and is fluent in Czech, German, Russian, and English. In 1972, Ivana was a member of the Czechoslovakian ski team, although she wasn't one of those chosen to compete in the Olympics in Sapporo, Japan. After the Olympics she went to Canada to stay with an aunt and uncle and became one of the top models in Montreal, while keeping her skiing up by serving as an instructor at Jay Peak in Vermont on weekends.

"Donald and Ivana are a close team," Boyle wrote. "Before he bought the Generals, he and his wife talked it over, because, as she says, 'Owning a football team means the end of our Sundays.'

THE BUILDING OF AN EMPIRE

Ivana herself designed the Generals' cheerleaders' new uniforms, which she thinks are 'fantastic.' ''

Since their marriage in 1977, a lot has changed in the Trump household, from their choice of homes, to their three children, Ivanka, Eric, and Donny. Ivanka, the oldest of the three Trump children, is now of kindergarten age, and Donald mentioned that event in his autobiography. ''I go with Ivana to look at a private school for my daughter. If you had told me five years ago that I'd be spending mornings looking for kindergarten classrooms, I would have laughed.''

Then, two days later, he writes, ''Ivana rings. She's in the office and wants me to go with her to see another school we're considering sending our daughter to next fall. 'Come on, Donald,' she says. 'You haven't got anything else to do.' Sometimes I think she really means it.''

Donald's love for his wife and family are more than apparent, when he chooses to set aside his important work, to accompany Ivana. ''Actually, honey, I'm a little busy right now,'' he tells Ivana half humorously. ''It doesn't work,'' he writes. ''Three minutes later she's in my office, tugging at my sleeve. I finish signing the forms, and we go.''

Ivana's strong personal convictions and courage to speak her mind have become somewhat of a trademark with her. While some describe her as a ''Bengal tiger,'' others see her as a competent and meticulous individual. Donald calls her ''demanding and competitive.'' Ivana's abilities as a design coordinator proved her professional mettle, and Donald Trump began to share his professional responsibilities with her more and more.

"Almost immediately,'' Donald said, after his marriage to Ivana, ''I gave her responsibility for the interior decorating on the projects I had under way. She did a great job.

"Ivana may be the most organized person I know,'' Mr. Trump says proudly. ''In addition to raising our three children, she runs our three homes—the apartment in Trump Tower, Mar-a-lago, and our home in Greenwich, Connecticut— and now she manages Trump's Castle, which has approximately 4,000 employees.''

Donald put Ivana in charge of the Castle because he wanted someone in the CEO position that was competent and someone he knew that he could trust implicitly with every aspect of the casino's operation. Maggie Mahar wrote about Ivana's work at Trump's Castle, in *Barron*'s: ''Ivana Trump spends four days a week at Trump's Castle, signing every check, and inspects every vendor's bill. She takes note of daily slot revenues, questions any drop in cash flow and can recite the most obscure details: For instance, that the average car that comes to her garage brings 2.3 passengers.'' One employee noted that, ''She knows it's her money.''

"The Castle is doing great,'' notes Mr. Trump,

"but I still give Ivana a hard time about the fact that it's not yet number one." In fact, at the moment (1988), Trump's Castle, in the firm control of Ivana Trump, is the number one money making casino in Atlantic City, and has been for many months. "I tell her she's got the biggest facility in town," Trump writes, "so by all rights it should be the most profitable. Ivana is almost as competitive as I am and she insists she's at a disadvantage with the Castle. She says she needs more suites. She isn't concerned that building the suites will cost $40 million. All she knows is that not having them is hurting her business and making it tougher for her to be number one. I'll say this much: I wouldn't bet against her."

Ivana's presence in the fine operations run by the Trump Organization, was well established long before she took charge of Trump's Castle. When Donald Trump bought into the Grand Hyatt Hotel, he found that he was forced to sit back as half owner of the operation, while the other half dealt with the entire management. In Donald's words, "Hyatt's job was to manage the hotel, so my role was essentially over. But the fact is I still had a 50 percent interest, and I'm not exactly the hands-off type. I would send over one of my executives, or more often my wife, just to see how things were going, and Hyatt wasn't happy about that. One day I got a call from the head of all the Hyatt Hotels, Patrick Foley, and he said, 'Donald, we have a problem. The manager of the hotel is going nuts, because your wife comes by, and she'll see dust in the corner of the lobby and call over a porter to clean it up. Or she'll see a doorman in a uniform that's not pressed, and she'll tell him to get it cleaned.' ''

The fact that Ivana treats every Trump operation, as if it were her own, led Donald to believe that she should have much more control. To Ivana's credit, she has proved time and time again that her interests do not lie solely on being just the wife of Donald Trump.

"Ivana," writes Donald, "is a great manager who treats her employees very well, but she's also very demanding and competitive. Her employees respect her because they know she's pushing herself as hard as she's pushing them.

"Rather than hire an outside general manager," Mr. Trump says about Trump's Castle, "I decided to put my wife, Ivana, in charge. I'd studied Atlantic City long enough to be convinced that when it comes to running a casino, good management skills are as important as specific gaming experience. She proved me right."

But for a few slight problems at the beginning of Trump's stake in Trump's Castle, he says that "The story of Trump's Castle has been almost entirely a positive one. Much of the credit has to go to Ivana. No detail escapes her. She has systematically hired the best people in Atlantic City at all levels—from croupiers to hosts to her top executives. She oversaw the decoration of the hotel's public spaces, which are now quite spectacular. The facility is always spotless, because she's meticulous even about that. And,'' Mr. Trump says firmly, ''great management pays off. It pays to trust your instincts.

''When the figures were announced for the first three months of 1987,'' Trump announced, ''Trump's Castle had the biggest increase in revenues among all of the twelve casinos in Atlantic City and was the most profitable hotel in town. The Castle took in $76.8 million in those three months—a 19 percent gain over the comparable period during the previous year. Good as that performance is, there is no way Ivana will be happy until she's outdistanced the field.''

The title of Chief Executive Officer, is much more than a token title to appease Ivana. Her executive capabilities have been proved to their limit, and Ivana is truly a CEO to be reckoned with. Though Donald likes to joke that he pays Ivana, ''$1 and all the dresses she can wear,'' I'd say her contribution to the Trump Organization is worth considerably more. ''She's incredibly good at anything she's ever done,'' Donald admits fondly, ''a natural manager.''

James Norman of *Business Week*, calls Ivana, ''a whirlwind of energy.'' And according to Mr.

Norman, "she sends the Castle's keepers scurrying with orders."

"Then they spend the rest of the week cleaning up the mess," jokes one Trump employee.

Ivana has no bones about keeping the employees efficient and attentive to doing a quality job in her Castle. Like Donald, who says, "I like people to know I watch them closely," Ivana likes to make her presence known. Annetta Miller of Atlantic City, once wrote about Ivana in *Newsweek*. "At first her work for Trump's empire was confined to interior design. But when Donald opened the Castle in 1985, her horizons expanded. Today Ivana reigns over more than 3,500 employees. She has learned much from her developer husband— some might say too much. Like Donald, she has a reputation as a stern taskmaster. Those who incur her wrath are sometimes subjected to what one employee describes as 'the Bengal tiger' routine: 'When someone makes a mistake, she doesn't just say "tut-tut," she attacks.'

"That approach has gotten results," Ms. Miller wrote. "In the first three months of 1987, Trump's Castle posted operating profits of $18,227,000, making it the city's best performing casino. Ivana, who oversees everything from the hotel kitchen to the blackjack tables, likens her role to 'running a small city.' Her salary—$1 and all the dresses she wants, according to Donald—is OK with Ivana. 'Donald,' she explains, 'gave me my chance.' "

Ivana accompanies Donald both in the business world and in the social scene. The Trumps are often the subjects of social gossip, and celebrity profiles. Though they share a high profile image, both in fashion and business, they prefer to keep themselves distanced from those worlds, while they maintain a strong family grounding. Though one day you might read about the Trumps in the sports page, the next in the society columns, the next in a newspaper's business sections, and even the next day see them on "Lifestyles of the Rich and Famous," they always keep their family unit in check by spending as much time as allowed, with each other.

In a *New York Times Magazine* article, written by William E. Geist, the subject of the Trump family's attention to each other came up. "Mrs. Trump says that though they both work long hours, they try to spend two or three nights a week at home with the children, but the social obligations do pile up."

Mr. Trump can well understand the importance of maintaining strong family ties with his wife and children, having come from such a close knit family himself. Though Ivana was an only child, her experience with the family-like atmosphere of Olympic athletes has also enabled her to understand and appreciate the family unit as well.

Some of the incredible social events and obligations that the Trumps participate in would seem like the pastimes of royalty. Meeting with heads of state, important political hopefuls, and dining with the business leaders of our age would seem like a dream come true for most Americans. Not to say that the Trumps don't appreciate their associations with these prominent individuals, they do. Donald and Ivana have met with the President of the United States, Mayors of our biggest cities, and even Soviet officials. Their calendar must seem like a list of important political and social "Who's Who" with no end in sight.

Ivana often accompanies Donald Trump, be it dinner, fund raising events, or to foreign countries. In Trump's autobiography he mentions a dinner he and Ivana attended with John Cardinal O'Conner, one of the many and frequent meetings they have with the elite. "6:00 P.M. I excuse myself because I am due at an early dinner, and it's not the kind to be late for. Ivana and I have been invited by John Cardinal O'Conner to have dinner at St. Patrick's Cathedral.

"7:00 P.M. No matter whom you've met over the years, there is something incredible about sitting down to dinner with the cardinal and a half dozen of his top bishops and priests in a private dining room at St. Patrick's Cathedral. It's hard not to be a little awed.

"We talk about politics, the city, real estate, and a half dozen other subjects, and it's a fascinating evening. As we leave I tell Ivana how impressed I am with the cardinal. He's not only a man of great warmth, he's also a great business-man with great political instincts.'' The respect that Donald and Ivana hold for their position of prominence is obvious. They are not the least bit smug about their connections, and they are not embarrassed to admit it.

"In addition to dinner parties," Mr. Giest wrote, "Mrs. Trump says they like to attend Broadway openings and that they frequent the ballet and opera. Mrs. Trump is active in support of the United Cerebral Palsy Fund and other charities as well as the New York City Opera." The Trumps make no bones about giving vast amounts of their wealth to important charities. The need to help the unfortunate is as important to the Trumps as is running their businesses.

During a television interview with Larry King, Donald Trump was asked by a caller to comment on the charge that the Trumps haven't given quite enough of their money to charity, a subject that arose during a previous interview on Crossfire. The caller, a law student from Louisiana, said, "I'd like to ask you one question. How did you handle yourself with Tom Brady and Pat Buchanon, blasting you for not giving more of your personal income on Crossfire? I was watching with my family, and I was about to laugh because I didn't know how you were going to control yourself, and these people who probably don't give anything, were blasting you for not giving more millions than you already have.'' Mr. Trump's response was straight forward and honest. Ivana and Donald give as much of themselves as they do of their own money to many important and worthy charities, Mr. Trump responded. ''Well, I appreciate it very much, and good luck with your law school. Frankly, I enjoyed the show, they're both good men, we had a lot of fun, they did blast me, there's no question. But as you probably know, I've given million and millions and millions of dollars to charity, even as you know, the book, (*Trump, The Art of the Deal*) which is now number one, all the proceeds from that book go to charity. The proceeds from Wollman Rink go to charity, the proceeds from so many other things that I do go to charity. Last year and the year before I gave a million dollars to the Vietnam Veterans. So it's a little bit tough for me to sit back and listen to two people telling me about how I should give more when in one week, I've given more, I'm sure, than most people have given in their lifetime.''

The Trumps often go out of their way to give of themselves and their money to needy causes. Many times photos of Ivana and Donald have appeared in magazines and newspapers at charitable benefits, such as the Human Resources Celebrity Sports Nights, and many others. Though the two have never seemed to be actually hurting themselves, they both see the realities of the world, and are glad to be able to help the unfortunates who are. Larry King asked Mr. Trump, "How do you determine, Don, who you give to? How do people with wealth, make that determination, when the person comes to the door?"

"Well, I think it's just an instinct that you have to have," he responded honestly. He then stated that they, "give a lot of money to United Cerebral Palsy, to the Vietnam Veterans (Donald serves as cochairman of the Vietnam Veterans Memorial Commission) [and] to a number of other causes. I'm going to start very heavily now with the homeless, with AIDs research, and with other things. It's really a feeling that you develop for whatever charity it might be, and there are a lot of good ones out there. I think everybody has an obligation, especially people that have made a lot of money, I really feel that you have an obligation to put it back."

The Trumps don't restrict their help to charities. Sometimes just the fact that they can give people a solid job in the community, in one of their many businesses, is as important as merely donating funds. Still though, there is just so much a person can do, including Donald and Ivana Trump. Take for instance, the comments that the Trumps should pay for an airport renovation near their casinos in Atlantic City. Maggie Mahar's accusation concerning that very situation in *Barron*'s: "If Atlantic City is to move even further upscale, from stationwagons to planeloads of junketeers, casino promoters cite one evident need: a bigger and better place to set down a plane. The airport near town requires expansion. But even Donald Trump isn't expected to bulldoze the new runway soon." As if Donald Trump is responsible for the city's entire list of problems. Ivana felt compelled to respond to the assumption that she and husband Donald need to renovate the local airport. "This is something local government should do," she said truthfully. "We can give the people jobs, but there is a limit to what we can do for the people." Ms. Mahar was quick to pipe in, "Or what the Trumps want to invest."

It is common knowledge that gambling casino's major revenue sources are the small time bettor. The guy who comes into a casino and loses $5,000 isn't the major money source. It is the grandma from Pittsburgh or the couple from Poughkeepsie who pump twenty dollars into the slot machines, day after day, week after week, year after year, that bring millions of dollars into the major casinos. "People go to Las Vegas for big events—to get married, for an anniversary. They don't come here," concedes the lovely Mrs. Trump. "But we are so close to major cities that people come constantly for smaller vacations." Donald agrees that Atlantic City brings in visitors from all over the east coast but that doesn't exempt the fact that some problems are always prevelant. "Atlantic City," Mr. Trump once said, "has been very good. Any time you try the gambling experiment, a state or a city or a municipality, it's always a very very tough and strenuous thing for that municipality. It causes a lot of problems. It's really turmoil in a lot of ways. And that's why, when you look at the experiment, a lot of other states don't do it.

"And no other states do it except [Atlantic City, really, and] Nevada. But Atlantic City from the Trump stand point has been a very successful experiment. We've done a great job. We have two of the most successful hotel casinos in the world. Just recently we made a deal to take over Resorts International. We're building . . . I guess the most expensive building ever built. It's a $900 million dollar building called the Taj Mahal in Atlantic City, and I think when it's completed it'll be incredible," Mr. Trump said in his most confident tone.

"Atlantic City really has a great advantage, because we're right next to New York, we're right near Washington and Philadelphia. A lot more people can come down. You're really nearer the media center," Trump said, while adding, "There's more money to be made in Atlantic City than in Las Vegas."

"He has not yet indulged in planes, race cars, polo ponies, art work, yachts, and the like," William E. Geist said of Donald Trump in 1984, foreshadowing the purchase of his new helicopter in 1987. "He says he doesn't have the time for all of that now and prefers putting his money back into his deals. Of course there is that estate in Greenwich and Mrs. Trump says, 'We have a speed boat up there, and I like to go out and go a hundred miles an hour in it and come back. We don't want to sit on a yacht all day.' "

Admittedly, the Trumps are anything but layed back. When one indulges in the quick stepping world of high finance, time, and the ability to be on time, is a constant and major factor. This is one of the reasons Donald and Ivana Trump make good use of their five helicopters, and the new 727 airplane, which was recently acquired for a mere $8 million dollars.

"I finally found a plane," Mr. Trump wrote in his autobiography. "I happened to be reading an article in *Business Week* in the spring of 1987 about a troubled, Texas based company named Diamond Shamrock. The article described how top Shamrock executives were enjoying incredible perks, actually living like kings. Among the examples cited was a lavishly equipped company-owned 727, which the executives flew around in at will."

The Trump itch for a deal grabbed Mr. Trump, as it had many times before, and he set out to get the 727. His excitement was evident, as he described the deal. "I sensed an opportunity. On

Monday morning, I called the office of the Diamond Shamrock executive who had been pictured on the cover of *Business Week* article. It turned out that he was no longer there and a new chairman, Charles Blackburn, had just been named. I was immediately put through to him, we talked for a few minutes and I wished him well. Then I said that I'd read about the company's 727, and that if he had any interest in selling, I was interested in buying. Sure enough, Blackburn said that as much as they all loved that plane, selling it was one of the first things on his agenda. He even offered to send it up to New York, so that I could take a look at it.

"The next day I went out to La Guardia airport for a look. I had to smile. This plane could seat up to two hundred passengers, but it had been reconfigured for fifteen, and it included such luxuries as a bedroom, a full bath, and a separate working area. It was a little more plane than I needed, but I find it hard to resist a good deal when the opportunity presents itself.

"A new 727 sells for approximately $30 million. A G-4, which is one fourth the size, goes for about $18 million. However, I knew that Diamond Shamrock was hungry to sell, and that not many people are in the market for 727s."

Donald's ballsy approach won him the airplane, at a time when it would have been extremely difficult for Diamond Shamrock to find a buyer.

Donald made a rock bottom offer, which under any other circumstances, would have never been considered, a paltry five million dollars. "They countered at $10 million," Mr. Trump said, "and at that point I knew I had a great deal, regardless of how the negotiation ended. Still, I haggled some more, and we finally agreed on a price of $8 million." Donald Trump, triumphant once again, praised his new travel toy. "I don't believe there is any other private plane in the sky comparable to this one."

Mr. Trump's flying machines are always available for Ivana's use. She often flies in to New York, in one of the many private helicopters, from Atlantic City, and according to *Newsweek*, he even named one of his, Ivana.

In *Newsweek,* the reporters described a brief flight in one of the Trump choppers. "A huge black helicopter with red lettering—TRUMP—flutters above the southern tip of Manhattan. The French-made military chopper can travel 180 miles per hour; at $2 million, the price Trump paid Warner Communications for it, it was a steal. He is flying to Atlantic City to promote an upcoming heavyweight fight that his casino is sponsoring. With him is Don King, the bombastic boxing promoter and heavyweight champ of hair. It is a cloudless morning, and before banking to the southwest the pilot hangs the copter directly above the gleaming twin towers of the World Trade Center for half a minute. Neither Trump nor King pays much attention to the staggering view. A reporter is present, and it's showtime.''

When it is time for business, Donald Trump doesn't have time for casually enjoying the view of a city he's seen hundreds of times from the air. The boxing events at Trump's Castle are an important phase of the kind of blockbuster entertainment Trump has in mind for the entire Atlantic City operations. As mentioned elsewhere in this book, he is always on the lookout for huge and crowd pleasing events, and to change the stigma that Atlantic City is solely for small vacation oriented gambling.

With the help of Ivana Trump, and his ever positive approach, it should be no time at all, before Atlantic City becomes the world's best gambling and entertainment mecca. ''I like to kid her that she works harder than I do,'' Mr. Trump says of his fashionable wife. Sometimes Ivana does work as hard as Donald, in fact, she does it right by his side. The two went as a team to Moscow recently to seek a site for a possible hotel concession in the Soviet Union. Obviously, Ivana's Russian speaking abilities were a valued asset to the important negotiations in Moscow, and they impressed the Soviets to no end. It may be some time before the Trumps are allowed to build in Moscow, but when it does happen it will be worth the wait for Donald and Ivana Trump, the Soviet Union, and the American people.

Entrepreneur, industrialist, Armand Hammer wrote a brief story in his autobiography, *Hammer*, which gave light to doing business in the U.S.S.R. "In 'As I See It,' John Paul Getty tells a story about me," Mr. Hammer recalled. "Like everybody who is reputed to be wealthy, Paul was constantly besieged by people who wanted to snatch a piece of his fortune for themselves, or to learn 'the magic formula' for instant riches. It made him impatient to be nagged by people who insisted that there must be some 'secret' by which he had made his fortune—rather than the more obvious qualities of hard work, ingenuity, resourcefulness, and care."

I'm sure the same question comes up from time to time when Mr. Trump speaks with various people. "Paul remembered that I had once been approached at a party by somebody who had asked me the 'tell-me-the-secret-of-making-millions' question.

"According to his version, I furrowed my brow and said, 'Actually, there's nothing to it. You merely wait for a revolution in Russia. Then you pack all your warm clothes and go there. Once you've arrived, you start making the rounds of the government bureaus that are concerned with trade, with buying and selling. There probably won't be more than two or three hundred of them . . .' At this point my questioner angrily muttered something and turned away." Though Armand Hammer's first ascent into the Russian business world was in the twenties, the same reasoning is valid today for Mr. Trump's attempt at building in the Soviet Union. The new theories of Gorbachev's Glastnost policies, are somewhat of a revolution in themselves. Though the Trumps may have to go through years of bureaucratic dealings and cumbersome approvals, the timing is now perfect for him to enter, build, and win. The humorous explanation of Armand Hammer, shows new truth in an old way.

On the trip to Moscow with Ivana, Mr. Trump said upon his return, "It was an extraordinary experience. We toured a half dozen potential sites for a hotel, including several near Red Square. We stayed in Lenin's suite at the National Hotel, and I was impressed with the ambition of the Soviet officials to make a deal."

Not all of the press that Ivana and Donald receive is as good as the stories about their trip to Moscow. At times, the press chooses to ignore the really important events, and concentrates on the absurd. In "Ivana, the 'Queen of the Castle,' " an article about Ivana, Annetta Miller mentions some of that type of story. "The only place Ivana shows up more frequently than the boardroom these days is the social columns. This summer gossip columnists were abuzz with rumors of a feud between her and sister-in-law Blain Trump—the wife of Donald's younger brother Robert. Ivana calls the report 'totally nonsense.' In reality, any lack of warmth between the two women may be explained by their sharply different personalities. Blaine, the former Martha Lindley Blaine Beard Retchin, is a blue blood who dresses conservatively and 'is the kind of woman you might have grown up with,' says Jane Lane, an editor for *Woman's Wear Daily*; Ivana, the immigrant with a penchant for glitzy dressing, 'has more of a hard brilliance.'

''Glitzier is often better in the casino business—and Ivana's flashy taste has served her well. When a Castle designer suggests installing mirrored beds in the hotel's suites, Ivana is quick to approve. 'What the customer wants,'' she decrees, ''the customer gets.' ''

The article began by showing the strong points of Ivana's nature in dealing with the hotel/casino that she cares for so well. ''They're singing a new song in Trumpdom,'' the article begins. ''Advertisements for Trump's Castle and casino in Atlantic City used to feature the motto 'You're the King of the Castle.' But last month some of the ads got the royal flush. They were replaced by a slightly more liberated motto: 'You're the King and *Queen* of the Castle.' Casino officials say the change was prompted by complaints from women who felt snubbed by the slogan. Chief among them: Ivana Trump, wife of Donald, chief executive officer of his largest casino—and the real 'Queen of the Caste.'

"Blonde and statuesque, Ivana looks like she would be more at home on the pages of *Town & Country*, where she once was the subject of a lavish photo spread" (indeed a lavish photo spread, the story was a whopping twelve page piece), "at the Trumps' Mar-a-Lago estate in Palm Beach, Florida. But her origins are hardly those of the typical New York socialite.

"What's next for the Queen of the Castle? With her husband hinting at political aspirations, some believe *she* may be the one who has her sights on the White House. But Ivana sees a potential conflict: 'Can the First Lady run a casino?' "

And Ivana Trump runs a casino like no one else. She is not intimidated by her remaining competition either. When things seemed to be getting tense in Atlantic City, with every casino trying to lure the semi-active influx of gamblers to their own floors, Ivana said, "The cheesecake is getting sliced thinner. Only the strongest will survive." It was commendable of her to forewarn the competition.

Chapter 4
Trump's Tallest Achievements—
Can Anybody Do It?

"Can anybody do it?"
    —Larry King—

"I think you can. I think that people can attain, and by the way, everything's relative also, and you're not going to attain Manhattan success if you're living in a small town, generally speaking, but you can do it on a relative basis, and you can do it on a national basis. It's a lot of hard work, it's a lot of imagination, it's going forward, it's putting certain principles to work. It's really being the certain kind of a person that is going to be successful, and I think you can no matter where you live and no matter in what town you were brought up, because there are a lot of successful people out there, and they did it. A lot of those people came from small towns and they became very, very successful . . . In my opinion you can do well no

matter where you are. And, you know, you have to be flexible, you have to go with the punches, but you can do really well wherever you are, and small towns, a lot of advantages to small towns, and it's a beautiful lifestyle in many cases.''
—Donald Trump—

While working on the Grand Hyatt and convention center deals, Mr. Trump found a new project on the Bonwit Teller building, with the help of his financial assistant Louise Sunshine.

Since then he has amassed a vast fortune of real estate, casinos, pleasure and business vehicles, homes, and many other accomplishments under his belt. Once he'd tried his hand at spreading out, the limits before him seemed to diminish. With the reconstruction of the Commodore into the illustrious Grand Hyatt, Trump's credibility grew in the financial world. This reputation caused many a nay-sayer to change their opinions of Donald Trump.

"The Path to the Tower."

"An introduction from Mrs. Sunshine," wrote journalist Randall Smith, "helped ease Mr. Trump's way onto what is now the site of Trump Tower. Mr. Trump had long sought the location of the Bonwit Teller building, where real estate values are among the highest in the city, but for many years Genesco, Inc., Bonwit's corporate parent, expressed no interest. Mrs. Sunshine arranged an introduction to a large Genesco shareholder, who in turn arranged a meeting with Genesco's chairman, and Mr. Trump made the case. When Genesco subsequently sold the Bonwit chain of stores, Mr. Trump was offered a chance to buy the Bonwit lease for $25 million. He quickly arranged a letter of credit from Chase and snapped it up.''

Even in 1982, at the writing of the article, Mr. Trump had already captured the imagination of many people. His reputation in New York was as talked about in the upper circles as was other highly important people and events. ''*People* magazine and Rona Barret, the television celebrity journalist,'' Mr. Smith said, ''have gushed over the young promoter, and Mr. Trump courts such fame. He offers journalists rides in his Cadillac limousine and not-for-attribution tid-bits. He once crashed a press conference held by opponents of the hotel tax abatement and presented his own side, getting his side into news accounts and charming his opposition.

''Mr. Trump delights [in] putting his name on his projects. The not-yet-completed Trump Tower features a Broadway-style marquee with the name 'Trump Tower' bathed in lights. He named a restaurant at the Grand Hyatt 'Trumpets.' He insists such self-promotion is 'less of an ego thing than an economic thing. It adds value.'

''He is thus asking about 50 per cent more for units in the Trump Tower than the going rate at other luxury condominiums here. A one-bedroom

Trump condominium starts at $475,000, and prices rise to $5 million for a four-bedroom triplex.

"The sales pitch for the units includes an elaborate slide show and tapes of Frank Sinatra belting out 'New York, New York.' Mr. Trump doesn't encourage rumors about luminaries who will possibly live in his buildings.

"Both of Mr. Trump's buildings," Smith wrote, "are controversial testaments to his own style. Trump Tower has a saw-toothed facade that will be covered with bronze glass, and will include an enclosed shopping mall on six levels, as well as a five-story indoor waterfall. The Hyatt, built over the frame of the old Commodore Hotel, has a mirrored glass covering, which architect Der Scutt, who consulted on the building, says was needed to give 'an old building the image of something brand new.'

"Both buildings contrast with older neighboring ones, many of which are made of limestone, granite, or marble. Trump Tower is set to rise higher than either the new International Business Machines Co., headquarters on the same block or the new American Telephone & Telegraph Co., headquarters on the next. Trump Tower has been criticized as being too bulky and likely to contribute to mid-town congestion.

"A Tall Order. Tall as they are on the outside, they are even taller on the inside. Mr. Trump accomplished that magic by simply renumbering the floors. The first residential floor of Trump Tower, 20 stories about street level, is called the 30th floor. He defends the move, saying the lower floors are higher than usual. Hyatt's first floor of guest rooms, too, six stories up, is called the 14th floor. The architects on the Hyatt project say they resisted the inflated numbering as 'deceptive' and 'a form of hype,' but Hyatt backed its partner and the deed was done.

"Such promotional overstatement angers some of Mr. Trump's critics. Once, for example, he offered to waive what he called a $4.4 million broker's fee on the sale of the convention center site in order to have his father's name on the center. City officials checked, learned that the fee due was really only about $500,000 and declined. Mr. Trump says the commission 'should have been' $5 million, but he was later paid just under $600,000.

"Another time, he conditionally promised two art deco limestone friezes from the demolished Bonwit Teller building to a museum. Later, however, he said his own appraisers considered the two-ton items 'junk,' and his construction crew jackhammered the sculptures, causing one newspaper to blast him for 'aesthetic vandalism.'

"Underground Dispute. One city official says he will never negotiate with Mr. Trump again without a witness because 'he says so many things so fast it's hard to pin down what he actually said.' And [the] Metropolitan Transportation Authority has sued Mr. Trump over his allegedly unkept promises to help improve the Grand Central Subway station as part of the Hyatt project. Mr. Trump says he didn't do the work in question because the transportation authority later told him not to.

"As for the other incidents, he says they are a matter of interpretation. 'I pride myself on telling the truth,' Mr. Trump says. 'Everything I've said I was going to do, I've done.' Still, he concedes that he does on occasion play with the truth and exaggerate it for effect. 'I guess obviously there's a promotional element, whether or not I want it or realize it.'

"None of these criticisms show any sign of slowing down the young developer. He is planning an apartment building near Bloomingdale's, the popular department store, and an ambitious hotel condominium at Central Park South and Sixth Avenue, another prestigious location and now the site of the Barbazon Plaza Hotel. Perhaps the most logical extension of his show biz flash and glitter is the $175 million casino he is considering in Atlantic City, N.J.—but only if the town will build a new convention center."

Six short years later, Trump Tower is a huge success and considered a New York landmark, Trump Parc stands as an achievement of creativity and modern value, he is the largest casino owner/

operator in Atlantic City, and he owns some of the world's finest properties, including: *Trump Plaza* in Palm Beach, a twin tower waterfront condominium. (In the advertisements which promote the beautifully designed monument, which are shown in the pages of the *New York Times Magazine*, show a nubile female in a red and black swimsuit, lounging on a floatation mattress, floating in a sunlit, bluewater pool. Under the rectangular shot of the woman, is a smaller photo, in an upright rectangle, which not only shows Trump Plaza, but in placement makes up an interesting "T" design. The ad reads, "Our Palm Beach is so exciting, some people have to take it lying down."

"Exciting views. Nowhere else can you see it all. The ocean, Lake Worth, the whole of Palm Beach. And there's excitement in our double pools, our in-house restaurant, and our professional health club. Come see the exciting condominium choices at Trump Plaza, where Palm Beach comes to life.")

Actually, the place is fantastic. With only two apartments per floor, and starting price at around $300,000 (ranging on up to $1,800,000), it has a rare quality that many seek.

Mar-a-Lago. Trump's historically significant Florida estate. Mar-a-Lago, which Mr. Trump bought for an incredible $8 million, prompting a news flurry with headlines such as, "Mar-a-Lago's Bargain Basement Price Rocks Community," was the twenty acre estate of the late Marjorie Merriweather

Post, the Post cereals heiress, sits facing the Atlantic ocean and Lake Worth, and is estimated to be worth more than $30 million. "Buying Mar-a-Lago was a great deal even though I bought it to live in, not as a real estate investment," he wrote once.

Marjorie Merriweather Post built Mar-a-Lago in the early twenties, while she was married to Edward F. Hutton. It took four years before it was completed, and has some 118 rooms. "Three boatloads of Dorian stone dating back to the fifteenth century were used on the exterior and the interior," says Mr. Trump.

He gives a brief history of the spacious mansion. "When Mrs. Post died she gave the house to the federal government for use as a presidential retreat. The government eventually gave the house back to the Post Foundation, and the foundation put it up for sale at an asking price of $25 million. I first looked at Mar-a-Lago while vacationing in Palm Beach in 1982. Almost immediately I put in a bid of $15 million, and it was promptly rejected. Over the next few years, the foundation signed contracts with several other buyers at higher prices than I'd offered, only to have them fall through before closing. Each time that happened, I put in another bid, but always at a lower sum than before.

"Finally, in late 1985, I put in a cash offer of $5 million, plus another $3 million for the furnishings in the house. Apparently, the foundation was tired of broken deals. They accepted my offer, and we closed one month later."

It was only hours after the sale was closed, that the Palm Beach *Daily* ran the headline, "Mar-a-Lago's Bargain Basement Price Rocks Community."

"Soon," Trump says, "several more modest estates on property a fraction of Mar-a-Lago's size sold for prices in excess of $18 million. I've been told the furnishings in Mar-a-Lago alone are worth more than I paid for the house. It just shows that it pays to move quickly and decisively when the time is right. Upkeep of Mar-a-Lago, of course, isn't cheap. For what is costs each year, you could buy a beautiful home almost anywhere in America."

Mr. Trump "found" the twin towered condominium while staying at Mar-a-Lago and lunching with friends. Trump calls Mar-a-Lago his and Ivana's "winter home." On the grounds of the estate are a 9-hole golf course, guest and staff houses, swimming pool, tennis courts, greenhouse, and beautiful citrus groves.

Trump's Castle is one of the many enterprises that Mr. Trump has taken in close to heart. The $320 million hotel and casino in Atlantic City has been virtually the hottest spot in that city since his acquisition of it. Recently, Donald Trump paid an unprecedented fee of $11 million to acquire rights to the Michael Spinks and Mike Tyson fight scheduled for June 27, 1988. The fight is contingent on the success of Tyson's bout with Tony Tubbs scheduled for March 21 in Tokyo, Japan.

"The fighters want it, the promoters want it," Mr. Trump said of Atlantic City hosting the heavyweight bout over Las Vegas. "There's more money to be made in Atlantic City than Las Vegas. So I think we'll have a lot of advantages."

In his *Boxing Week* column expert Jack Fiske wrote the following opinion: "The Man With A Golden Arm Rolls Eleven. Eleven million dollars as a site fee for Mike Tyson vs. Michael Spinks is obscene, whether it's for Atlantic City or Las Vegas. I wonder how the homeless feel about it.

"Wednesday was a dual day of triumph for Atlantic City realtor/casino owner Donald Trump. Only hours before he bought the fight, Trump moved closer to becoming sole owner—at a drastically reduced $22 per share—of Resorts International on the boardwalk, his third Atlantic City hotel together with Trump Castle and Trump Plaza.

"In a move that insured eventual completion of the Taj Mahal—the crown jewel of Trump's properties—the New Jersey Casino Control Commission relicensed Resorts, after refusing a week earlier because the hotel had not fulfilled its commitment of 12 years ago to an Atlantic City housing and development fund. Trump previously had begged ignorance of the $20–$40 million commitment.

"Now he's got what promises to be the richest fight in history, but Trump is more concerned with the 'drop' the weekend of the fight, June 27.

"The 'drop' is what the casinos realize from high roller tourists and fight fans before and immediately after the fight. Trump's outlay of $11 million (plus incidentals for the promotion) almost certainly will be recouped from the live gate at Convention Center, to be upgraded from 18,000 seats to 21,000. Tickets will sell for $100 to $1,500."

Mr. Fiske then elaborated upon his views of Atlantic City's profit potential, saying that "Trump's claim that Atlantic City has supplanted Las Vegas as the fight capital of the world is premature. Quality fights (not quantity fights) and title fights (not necessarily big money fights) will determine the champion. So far, Atlantic City is merely a tough challenger, not the title holder."

Consider these, as some of Donald Trump's best acquisitions, but bear in mind that these are but a handful of his current projects, and that there are many more in the making, or in the deal stage. A recent article which appeared in the Los Angeles *Times*, written by Michael A. Hiltzik, attempted to provide the latest understanding of Mr. Trump's activities and accomplishments. "New York. On one side of the table was the head of a tenants committee and the group's aggressive grassroots lawyer. On the other side, Donald J. Trump, landlord, was airing out one of the most useful tools in his negotiating arsenal: his exceptionally ingratiating line of flattery.

" 'We met for [a] three or four hour lunch, and he spent the first two hours complimenting me,' recalled Donald Rosenholc, a lawyer who was more accustomed to dealing with thuggish slumlords than the blond, honey-tongued, expensively tailored developer of multi-million-dollar high-rise aeries.

"Rosenholc had fought Trump to a standstill over his attempt to evict the tenants of a distinguished old apartment house at 100 Central Park South in order to convert it into yet another brand-name luxury condo building. Trump's managers had let the building services deteriorate, stripping the lobby of even its Christmas tree and brought innocent tenants up on rent non-payment charges.

"As a result, the tenants stood to win a highly damaging and embarrassing harassment case against Trump.

"As negotiations dragged on, Rosenholc took the floor and shut down the river of flattery with a blunt expletive. Soon after that, Trump capitulated with a settlement that gave the tenants even more rights than they might have won under a city order.

"Not that Trump did not get in the last word. In his best selling book, *Trump: The Art of the Deal,* he dismissed the tenants as people 'for whom hardship is not being about to get a table on 30 minutes notice at Le Cirque,' New York's toniest restaurant.

"In any case," he wrote, "he eventually made more than $100 million for 100 Central Park South and the building next door.

"Thus did Donald Trump turn one of his few public relations disasters (*New York* magazine had featured the dispute under the headline, "A Different Donald Trump Story") into yet another self-congratulatory anecdote for his best-selling autobiography.

"Of course, no one would claim that Trump has ever been weak on self promotion. Since 1980, he has been New York's most visible and extravagant real estate man, plastering his name over Manhattan island like the label on a pair of designer jeans.

"Now the question on people's minds is whether Trump is preparing for a jump to the West Coast. What inspires the speculation is the announcement by MCA on Feb. 12 that Trump has disclosed a holding of $15 million of the huge entertainment conglomerate's stock (less than 1%) and was considering buying as much as 24.9%.

"Followers of the corporate raiding fraternity might not be so impressed, because in the course of making hundreds of millions of dollars on the stock of a handful of important hotel, gaming, and real estate companies during a two-year prowl of the stock market, he has only once mounted a genuine takeover. Some Trump followers speculate that he really has his eyes on MCA's generous holdings of real estate in Southern California and Florida.

"But it does appear that Trump's name can work its magic on the stock exchange as well as on the New York housing market: MCA shares have risen more than 15%, to $46.25, since the Feb. 12 disclosure.

"Trump has had close to a decade of experience in turning expectations and promotion into hard profits.

"On Fifth Avenue, Trump Tower, with its glittering glass appointments and glitzy pink marble retail lobby, has long since replaced the staid marble mansions and apartment houses a few blocks further uptown as the popular symbol of luxury living. Across town, Trump Plaza has helped convert the upper East Side from a neighborhood of townhouses and middle class apartment blocks into an overbuilt community of high-rise *pied-a-terres*.

"Moving afield, Trump stands likely to become the largest casino owner in Atlantic City, N.J., where his Trump Plaza and Trump Castle casinos are among the town's most heavily marketed and most successful. And now the developer, an owner of the New Jersey Generals of the defunct United States Football League (and moving force behind its ill-starred plan to compete on an autumn football schedule), is expressing interest in a bid for ownership of the NFL's troubled New England Patriots.''

Mr. Trump's attempt to purchase the Pats was mentioned in many newspapers from the New York *Times*, to the San Francisco *Chronicle*, to the Los Angeles *Times*. The *Times* reported, ''Dedham, Mass., Feb. 16 (AP)—Donald Trump, the New York real estate magnate and one of the principal voices in the defunct United States Football League, was added today to the roster of potential buyers for the New England Patriots.

''The attorneys for the financially strapped Sullivan family, owners of the Patriots, said that talks had been held with Trump, who owned the New Jersey Generals in the U.S.F.L. Attorneys for a group headed by Fran Murray of Philadelphia, which holds an option to buy the team, also confirmed the discussions.

'' 'Donald Trump is interested in the New England Patriots,' Joel Kozol, attorney for the Sullivans, said today after a hearing in Norfolk Superior Court involving the Patriots' financial situation was postponed for at least one day. 'He's made an absolute commitment that the team would stay in New England, and that would be part of any deal that is made.'

''Trump's office had no immediate comment,'' the story read. ''But his talks with the Patriots are not the first he has had about a National Football League team. During the U.S.F.L.–N.F.L. antitrust suit, both Trump and Commissioner Pete Rozelle of the N.F.L. testified that Trump had expressed interest in buying the Baltimore Colts in the late 1970's and early 1980's. The Colts later moved to Indianapolis.

"If an agreement is reached with Trump, it would be subject to the approval of N.F.L. owners, most of whom saw Trump as their main antagonist during the fight with the U.S.F.L. The league disbanded after it was awarded just $1—trebled to $3 under antitrust laws—in its suit against the N.F.L., an award now under appeal.

"However, Art Modell, owner of the Cleveland Browns, said today he would be less interested in the personal animosity involved than the structure of the deal."

"At Trump Tower," writes Michael Hiltzik, "nestled in a corner spot on Fifth Avenue next door to Tiffany's, condominium apartments sell for as much as 25% more than equivalent units in other high-grade mid-town buildings, and 74% are purchased by corporations and non-resident investors.

"If Trump has made a name in Manhattan, the place where he has truly made his mark is Atlantic City. He moved into the fledgling gambling city in 1978, while the Commodore reconstruction was under way, and took the unusual but prudent step of applying for and receiving a casino license before beginning work on a casino hotel. The idea, he explained in a 1985 interview, was to prevent New Jersey authorities from insisting on costly changes on pain of withholding a license.

"Trump won his license partly by exercising the self-confidence that has since become familiar to followers of the rich and famous everywhere.

"His project, he told the Casino Commission, would be 'a big step for Atlantic City' because the resort town 'needs some pizazz.'

"Trump began construction of his first casino without a financial partner; after he spent slightly less than $50 million, Holiday Inns in 1982 bought a 50% equity interest in the project for its Harrah's subsidiary. The deal repaid all of Trump's expenditures, covered all further costs and left him with a 50% interest.

"Soon after that, he got a second big break in Atlantic City. Hilton Hotels, which had responded disdainfully to the state gaming commission's questions about its relationship with reputed mob lawyer Sidney Korshak, was unexpectedly denied a license for its almost completed Atlantic City casino-hotel."

Mr. Trump has denied any personal experience or knowledge of "mafia" types around his Atlantic City operations. A caller from North Carolina asked Mr. Trump about the existence of a "mafia," while on the Larry King live broadcast.

"I was wondering if there is a 'mafia,' how do you keep them out of the casinos you have. And the next question, what state do you think casinos will be in next?''

Trump responded, ''Well I think we have a very good system in Atlantic City. We have a very strong casino control commission, and it's a very highly regulated state. I've never seen any evidence of the 'mafia' per se, and I'm sure it exists, or whatever. I mean you just pick up a newspaper, and I assume you have to say it exists. But we have a very very strong regulatory process, and the Casino Control Commission in Atlantic City, in New Jersey, does a very good job. As far as other states, I don't see it in other states, because frankly, it's very negative. It's very negative in a lot of ways. The casino gambling experiment is a very negative experiment, and a lot of states that were thinking about it, after studying all the options, have decided not to go with it.

''It produces income and it produces problems, and the overall problems most people feel are far greater than the income and therefore they are saying, 'let's take a pass.' ''

Trump says that he wouldn't recommend trying casino operations in New York, ''because New York has enough problems. I mean, New York is doing very well,'' he says, catching himself, ''I mean when you look at New York, when you look at the tax rates, when you look at other things that are happening in New York, New York and especially Manhattan and New York City, they're doing so well, that they don't need anything else. They don't need the stimulous. But the fact is, the casino-gaming experiment has been a rough one, for every state, for any state that's looked at it, and that's why most of them, Florida just turned it down overwhelmingly, most of them after looking at the evidence have said no.''

''Trump blames Barron Hilton, the chain's chairman and the son of founder Conrad Hilton, for allowing the company to grow lax,'' writes Hiltzik on how Trump acquired the Hilton in Atlantic City for himself. '' 'You hear the name Hilton and you think of the legendary Conrad Hilton, but Barron is not from the same cloth,' Trump said in an interview. 'He was a member of the lucky sperm club.'

''In any event, Hilton's loss was Trump's gain; he took the costly casino off the company's hands virtually at cost and reopened it so fast that the Hilton name was still imprinted on the slot machines. Today, known as Trump Castle, its revenue growth has consistently remained among the top five of Atlantic City's 12 casinos.

''Soon after the Hilton acquisition, Trump bought out Holiday Inns' share of their partnership. Holiday Inns, appalled at the prospect of its own Atlantic City partner opening a second, competing casino, at first tried to enjoin Trump from putting his own name on the Hilton property. In exchange, Trump began to snipe at Harrah's management of the jointly owned casino—a surprising turnaround from his lavish praise of the management during the period when Harrah's Trump Plaza was the two partners' only property in town.''

Michael A. Hiltzik says that ''Sometimes his (Trump) incessant outflow of self promotion, extravagance and hyperbole runs a little thin.

''For one thing,'' Hiltzik says, ''having his own autobiography on the New York *Times* best-seller list provides him with the luxury of writing his own history.

''Take the book's version of the dispute at 100 Central Park South. At the time, Trump had battled tenants in part by vilifying them as wealthy parasites benefiting from state-regulated below-market rents while worthy middle class apartment hunters went begging. His most controversial move was to offer, as a public service, to donate a few of the buildings' vacant apartments to the city as housing for the homeless.

'' 'I genuinely felt it was a shame not to use a few vacant apartments when the streets were filled with homeless people,' he later wrote in the book. When the city demurred, he boarded up the vacant windows so the building looked like a misplaced Harlem tenement.

''Rosenholc has a different gloss on the proposal: 'There isn't anybody in America who believed that was a good faith proposal. It was simply harassment.'

"One agency whose patience with Trump has come close to running out is the New Jersey Casino Control Commission, which recently threw a wrench into his plans to complete and operate Atlantic City's largest casino, which would make him the city's biggest gambling kingpin and bring him to the maximum of three casinos that can be owned by any one entity.

"At issue," Hiltzik ranted, "was the so-called Taj Mahal, a vast hotel and casino complex begun by Resorts International but stalled since the death in April, 1986, of its chairman and controlling shareholder, James Crosby.

"From Crosby's survivors, Trump last year acquired a controlling interest in Resorts, but then engaged in months of bluster and threats to win the company board's approval for a complete takeover. Meanwhile, he tried to browbeat the casino commission into approving a multi-million dollar management contract paying him to complete the Taj Mahal—on one occasion suggesting that he might take Resorts into bankruptcy if it were not approved.

"Finally, on Feb. 18, two of the five commissioners—enough to deny the Taj Mahal a casino license—rebelled.

"Questioning whether Trump and his aides had treated the commission with 'honesty and integrity' during the eight-month licensing process, Commissioner Valerie H. Armstrong suggested that

Trump's blustering and hand-wringing over the condition of Resorts had 'been carefully staged, manipulated and orchestrated to drive down the value of (Resorts) stock' in order to allow him to more easily take over the company.

"She also complained that Trump had backpedaled on Resort's previous commitments to Atlantic City to build low- and middle-income housing on an urban-renewal tract as a condition of its casino license—a commitment demanded of all casino developers and honored mostly in the breach.

"Reputation mixed. The commission required that Trump appear for two days of hearings last week in which he was closely questioned . . . about his plans for management of Resorts International.

"After that, and after he agreed to the housing commitment, the commission approved a one-year extension of the Resorts license.

"Resorts not withstanding, Trump's reputation as a corporate raider is decidedly mixed. True, he has almost invariably racked up large profits from short-term holdings in such companies as Holiday Inns ($35 million), Allegis ($80 million), and Bally ($31.7 million). But the Bally profits carry the unmistakable emerald glow of greenmail.

"For his part, Trump stands by his claims that most of his forays into large block holdings in companies have been for investment only.

" 'Imagine . . . I buy some stock in Holiday

Inns,' he said. 'I buy 5%, I'm sitting at my desk, bought it for investment reasons, and all of a sudden you see the company enacting all sorts of [defensive moves] that do nothing and in this case drive the stock through the roof. So I say, 'Sell the stock.' It's amazing.'

"Trump made his $35-million profit on Holiday Inns by selling his bloc on the open market, thus getting the same price per share available to any investor. But the Bally deal was different.

"Trump paid an average $17 for each of his roughly 3.1 million shares.

"He resold 2.6 million shares to Bally last February for $24 each, not including an added $6.2 million sweetener to cover his litigation costs, at a time when the public market for Bally was just under $20 a share.

"He retained the right to sell his remaining 457,000 shares to Bally this year at $33 each. Deals like that, in which a company pays an investor a premium to repurchase his shares, are generally damned by Wall Street as an expense to the company and an injury to other shareholders.

"At the same time, many of Trump's stock campaigns have the taint of personal affairs. He accumulated his stock in Holiday Inns after his acrid disagreement with its Harrah's unit over the Trump Plaza partnership. More to the point, he also began accumulating stock in Golden Nugget, another one-time Atlantic City casino owner, after a number of run-ins with that company's impeccably groomed chairman, Steve Wynn.

"In his book, Trump gave Wynn the back of his hand: 'He's a smooth talker, he's perfectly manicured and invariably dressed to kill,' he wrote. 'The problem with Wynn is that he tries too hard to look perfect, and a lot of people are put off by him.'

"One is certainly Trump. Late in his negotiations with Hilton over the Atlantic City property, Trump learned that Wynn was bidding against him and threatening his deal. When he was rattling his saber in Bally stock, that company set the stage for his buyout by purchasing Golden Nugget's Atlantic City casino. By giving Bally two casinos in the city, the move meant that Trump—also the owner of two—would violate the state's ownership limit of three if he won control of Bally's;

"So Trump's announcement last July that he owned 4.9% of Nugget stock may have been designed just to aggravate Wynn, who in any event controlled directly and indirectly a commanding 40% of the company.

"Dispute with Koch. It is not unusual for Trump to engage in even more public disputes. Take his running battle with New York Mayor Edward I. Koch. The disagreement erupted last year over Trump's most grandiose proposal—a hundred acre development on a riverfront site that is Manhattan's largest underdeveloped piece of property.

Trump, who had long since christened the project 'Television City,' needed special city tax abatements to attract a prime tenant—the NBC television network, whose huge office and studio lease at Rockefeller Center is soon to expire.

"Koch refused to grant the subsidy and worked to keep NBC in Rockefeller Center. That led to the improbable spectacle of the city's leading developer calling the mayor a 'moron' and the mayor responding with the epithet 'piggy, piggy, piggy.' "

James Flanigan wrote about Trump's apparent takeover attempt, saying that "It won't lead to a takeover or much of anything really, but the flurry that Donald Trump is causing in the stock of MCA should alert people to the values and potential in what may be the fastest-growing global industry—entertainment.

"Trump, the highly publicized developer of glitzy New York buildings and Atlantic City casinos, filed a statement with the government last week declaring his intentions to acquire up to 18 million MCA shares, or 24.9% of the company.

"Meanwhile, however," Flanigan wrote, "Trump said he owns only 375,000 shares, or less than 1% of the company. And Wall Street arbitrageurs and analysts were skeptical that his declaration of intent was anything more than talk. Even though it was conceded that Trump could appreciate the value of MCA's real estate—as much as $2 billion worth in Los Angeles and Orlando, Fla., says analyst Mara Balsbaugh of the Smith Barney, Harris Upham brokerage—few gave the developer much chance of forcing MCA into a merger or reconstructing.

"Markets are exploding. In Europe, where governments used to control all television, many channels have gone private, and the demand for programming is growing—along with the prices the European buyers are willing to pay for old American movies and television shows. A series such as 'Magnum P.I.' may now hope to bring $250,000 an episode in worldwide syndication where such programming brought much less than $100,000. And TV expert Les Brown of *Channels* magazine predicts further rapid growth in Europe and in much of Asia—with particular emphasis on Japan, where the home video market is booming.

"It may seem unusual to talk of TV cop shows and old movies as a global industry—but it's perfectly reasonable when you think about it. What, after all, do the world's mass markets want in an age when development is spreading, there are more television sets in practically every country and people have more time? From the suburbs of Paris to the outskirts of Taipei, televisions are on for more hours of the day now. And that means a need for programming to fill the airtime, which means of course opportunity for the world leader in programming: Hollywood.

"So hooray for Hollywood. What does that specifically have to do with MCA? Just this. MCA has one of the largest film libraries in Hollywood and practically the largest library of television programs—oldies but goodies like 'Columbo' and 'Kojak'; newer ones like 'Murder She Wrote' and 'Miami Vice.' Some experts estimate the value of MCA's store of films could approach $3 billion.

"Talk like that, about real estate and film assets in the billions, may make people like Trump think of a takeover. But a takeover of MCA is extremely unlikely."

Flanigan says that MCA has made many "friends" over the years, and a hostile takeover is unlikely. There are too many options for MCA to allow just any takeover.

The Japanese, for instance, are a prime candidate for helping MCA in such an event. "Just last month," Flanigan writes, "MCA formed a joint venture with Nippon Steel to develop a Universal Studios Tour theme park in Japan. MCA and Nippon, the world's third largest steel company and a major Japanese land holder, said they would also explore other ventures in the entertainment field."

Chapter 5
The Trump Series—Executive and Golden Edition limousines

"Donald J. Trump . . . a name that has captured the admiration and imagination of New York City. Now, his fame extends world-wide.

"The name is synonymous with the word 'unique.' His organization is dynamic, his projects world class, and his locations superb. All testimonials to his imagination, daring, and architectural vision.

"There is little wonder that Cadillac, Donald Trump, and Dillinger Coach Works have collaborated to produce a unique 'Trump Series' of limousines. A singular match-up of extraordinary talent and style."

—From The Trump Series, information document—

Without a doubt, within his area of interest, Donald Trump has done more, and is the best at what he does than any other. The heights reached by Mr. Trump far exceed his profession, and he now finds parts of himself in a variety of different deals. Though his unseemingly related deals are as divergent as the man himself, they do relate to his business.

"The executive vice president for marketing at the Cadillac Division of General Motors is on the phone," Mr. Trump said toward the beginning of his popular book. "He's calling at the suggestion of his boss, John Gretenberger, the president of the Cadillac Motors Division whom I know from Palm Beach. Cadillac, it turns out, is interested in cooperating in the production of a new superstretch limousine that would be named the Trump Golden Series. I like the idea."

Then toward the end of the book, Mr. Trump proudly announced the culmination of the project. "A decision has been made to go into production on two Cadillac-body limousines using my name. The Trump Golden Series will be the most opulent stretch limousine made. The Trump Executive Series, will be a slightly less lavish version of the same car. Neither one has yet come off the line, but the folks at Cadillac Motors Divisions recently sent over a beautiful gold Allante as a gift. Perhaps they felt I needed more toys to keep me busy."

As of January 13, 1988, Donald Trump received the very first of the Trump Golden Series deluxe limousines for his private use. The super stretch exotic limousines are definitely the cream of the limousine crop. Bruce S. Cirlin, vice president of sales for the Dillinger/Gaines national leasing company, who both produce and distribute the new limousine, was kind enough to supply me with informational materials concerning the huge automobile.

"The word 'limousine,' " the promotional document begins, "takes on a new dimension with The Golden Edition, as pictured in Cadillac's national catalog. It represents the finest in luxury limousine travel. This limousine was designed, built and accoutred for those with the most exacting standards.

"Dillinger Coach Works, distinguished for building masterpiece limousines, has reached unsurpassed heights with the Golden Edition. This limousine stretches 60″ beyond the base length of the Cadillac Brougham. Distinctive to its exterior profile is a customized raised grill adorned with the gold plated Cadillac identification. Another prominent feature is its vertically patterned grill."

As soon as the press heard of the Trump Golden Edition, the airwaves were abuzz with comments. The story was covered daily by such networks as CNN in January 1988. Reporter Beverly Shook covered the story. "What does Cadillac and real estate mogul extraodinaire Donald Trump have in common? A car, or rather a new breed of limousine, for the privileged and pampered executive.

"Cadillac, with 60% of the limousine market,

and Trump, a master of marketing, say they have found a neglected niche.

"This one," Ms. Shook said of the Trump Golden Series, "has 24 carat gold plated antenna and seat belts strapped to Milano Italian leather seats. Standard features include TV, bar, and VCR, all remote controlled. A state of the art overhead comfort control system, faxcimile machine, and paper shredder.

"Besides a little luxury, as Dan Daily says, it's a practical machine as well. 'Instead of driving around and having unproductive time, they can have productive time, while they're going home, or while they're going to a meeting or whatever,' says Dan Daily of Dillinger Coach Works."

For obvious reasons, Cadillac and Dillinger Coach works are unquestionably proud of their latest and most fantastic design. "Tracing the expanse from bumper to bumper is a hand painted gold pinstripe detailing the limousine's sleek contour. Upscale authentic wire wheels are fitted with gold striped tires by Vogue. Cruising at high speeds, The Golden Edition is seductively silent; its passenger cabin uncommonly tranquil. Premier aircraft insulation adds to its peaceful ride while tinted windows lend an aura of complete privacy. The Golden Edition of the Trump Series represents the ultimate."

The interior of The Golden Edition, is as elegant as the exterior. The accomadations exemplify the term luxury. "Open the door and revel in the sumptuous feel of the exquisite Milano Italian leather. Passengers, and chauffeur, are surrounded by soft supple seats framed with rich rosewood veneer panels. The fragrance of fine genuine leather permeates the cabin which seats five comfortably. The coup de grace is the 24 carat appointments.

"The entertainment center is complete with a compact disc player and a remote control television, AM/FM stereo with cassette and VHS cassette recorder. Combine all of this with an electronic wet bar, soda dispenser, and lead crystal beverage set—and the temptation to relax is overpowering.

"Within arms length is a cellular telephone with duel handsets and an overhead electronically controlled environmental system which also operates the astroroof. Other functional features include: dual pull-out desks, paper shredder, 110 volt electrical outlet, hands free intercom to the chauffer's compartment and a hidden safe.

"The Golden Edition tolerates no compromise in quality. Its design and performance are uniquely unparalled."

The Golden Edition surely represents the very height of excellence that Donald Trump expects in any of his ventures. With his assistance, The Golden Edition has become the ultimate in preferential travel, as the Trump buildings represent the very best architectural design. "Plush passenger seats made of fine Milano Italian leather are a prominent feature in this luxurious limousine. The gold

Cadillac/Trump emblem embroidered into the seats is an unspoken confirmation of quality and excellence. The two beautifully styled pull-out writing desks are easily accessible for passengers' needs. And behind the rear passenger seat is a paper shredder positioned next to the flexible gooseneck reading lamp. The abundance of 24 carat gold plated accoutrements provide a dramatic contrast to the dark interior and the tinted glass enhances its privacy. Communication features include a cellular telephone with two handsets positioned in the side wood panels and an intercom system controlled by a button located on the door panel.

"One hundred percent wool carpeting provides elegance and durability for this luxurious interior. The richly grained rosewood veneer finish console houses a premium audiovisual system with a Blaupunkt AM/FM cassette wireless remote control stereo, Blaupunkt compact disc player and equalizer, and Sony wireless remote control television in a separate enclosed unit.

"Complimenting this fully electronic entertainment system is a Panasonic wireless remote control VHS video cassette recorder positioned at floor level under the rear-facing passenger seat. Inconspicuously located at floor level beside the cassette recorder is a 110 volt electrical outlet. Beautifully inlaid into the raised roof is the automatic glass panel. Located behind the passenger seat is a dual partition made of tinted glass or rosewood veneer.

"Elegant lead crystal decanters and matching glasses are a part of the enclosed console unit which also houses the remote control television.

"State-of-the-art electronic overhead comfort control system features digital temperature read out as well as control of door locks, astroroof, tinted glass or rosewood veneer privacy partition, and floor, dome, or mood lighting."

After all that one might think that the less expensive model, the Trump Executive Series, would be far less lavish. Not so. The Executive Series offers many of the same options, the only striking difference are the seats, less expensive electronic equipment, and of course, the 24 carat accents. The Executive Edition limousine is no less spectacular than the Golden Edition, with the exception of a few small differences, and except for the Golden Edition, it is possibly the very best available.

"Functional elegance aptly describes The Executive. This limousine is expressly crafted for one who is geared to transforming commuting time into productive time.

"Certainly its appearance does not convey an all-business façade. It, too, has a raised grill with patterned formal vertical lines and extends 60″ beyond the base of the Cadillac Brougham.

"The Executive's appearance is accented by the red pinstripes, deluxe wire wheel covers and whitewall tires. Again, tinted glass is called upon for the element of privacy. The plush interior includes burgundy velour seating, genuine rosewood veneer, electronic wet bar, lead crystal beverage set, and an extensive entertainment center. There is no question of this limousine's uncompromising elegance.

"The plush burgundy velour seats, embroidered with the Cadillac/Trump emblem, comfortably accomodate five passengers. Inconspicuously located in the armrest is a safe in which important items may be stored. On either side of the built-in tissue holder are flexible gooseneck reading lamps. For immediate contact with the chauffeur's cabin, an intercom system is controlled by a button above the door handle. The tinted windows, while offering privacy, add to this limousine's dramatic effect."

As with the Golden Series, The Executive Series offers 100% wool carpeting which, according to Dillinger Coach Works, "provides elegance and durability," to the Executive's plush interior.

"The custom wood package includes an elegant rosewood veneer finish console in which is set a complete audiovisual system as well as convenient storage compartments. The Panasonic wireless remote control VHS video cassette recorder, Sony AM/FM stereo cassette deck, and Sony wireless remote control television combine as a complete entertainment and communication system. Elegant lead crystal glasses and decanters serve as accoutrements for the fully automatic Perm-A-Pub wet bar. Beautifully inlaid into the raised roof is a fully automatic glass panel. Hidden overhead are the conveniently placed vanity mirrors, opera lights and four corner overhead spot lights. Separating the passenger and chauffeur cabins in a dual partition of either tinted glass or rosewood.''

Some of the spectacular specifications of the two Trump Series Cadillac limousines, aren't to be found on any others. With a 283.2 inch length, 72 inch width, and 59 inch height, these massive limousines weigh in at a whopping 5626 pounds. The height is adjustable by electronic control, and the 255 horsepower engine sets the automobiles cruising in a matter of seconds. The limousines each boast two Delco-GM Freedom (R) 11-Plus dual [12 volt] batteries and a 94 amp generator with battery isolator. There is also 19.5 cubic feet of trunk space.

Beverly Shook: ''Trump will be the first to judge the new standard of opulance when he accepts the premier Trump Edition Cadillac. Dillinger Coach Works, who is custom building the car for GM's Cadillac Division, expects to knock off more than 200 cars this year. Each car comes with a $70,000 price tag, but Trump says the issue is 'quality,' and along with his name emblazoned on each limo, he'll get a royalty for each car sold. He won't say how much, but he says the money will go to charity.''

To date, these are the finest executive limousines ever conceived, and the top-of-the-line product will be used by the nation's most prominent businessmen. You can probably bet that Ed Koch won't be caught riding in one, but there are plenty of powerful executives that will.

"There's a good market for that," Trump states. "Cadillac wanted me to do it, and design it, and they wanted to put my name on it. I was honored, but more importantly than being honored, I needed them also. Because like everybody else, you just can't get a great limousine."

As with any radically new concept, the Golden Edition, and the Executive Edition Series will grow and adapt with the needs of the user. Expecting future modifications, Dillinger Coach Works notes that "the current specifications for this concept vehicle may change with the evolution of the concept."

To those of you who would cry if you had to own an Executive model ($55,000) instead of the more equipped Golden Series, a consoling thought: you won't get the paper shredder, but you will have a genuine, built-in rosewood veneer tissue holder, to help dry those tears.

Chapter 6
What People are Saying About Donald Trump

"I kind of like the idea of Donald Trump for President, but I think I have an even better idea—king."
—Matty Simmons, editor, *National Lampoon*—

Along with fame and recognition, also comes advice, threats, gossip, envy, and an assortment of offers and "old friends," crawling out of the woodwork. Once you are in the spotlight it is difficult to maintain any sort of anonimity. One gossip columnist will claim that you're having an alien's baby, or some devious person will say that you cheated him or her in some unsavory way, or even that every word that you say is a lie. It all comes with the territory.

Mr. Trump has had his share of weird requests and accusations, some good and some bad. The name, Trump, strikes a chord wherever it is spoken. The name is as familiar to a New York banker as it is to an eighteen-year-old up and coming landowner in the fields of Iowa. His name comes up in every major newspaper, appears along with his face on television programs like "Lifestyles of the Rich and Famous," and his face has graced the covers of almost every major magazine in this country. The prominence of the Trump title causes people to speak out, whatever their feelings of him. From the small town carpenter who says, "This guy's nuts! If I had that kind of money . . ." to the CEOs of big business, everybody has something to say about Donald Trump. Here are some of the things people are saying.

In a humorous quiz, offered by Colin McEnroe, an attempt at showing the permanence of Donald Trump's real estate holdings:

"According to a startling new theory unveiled by scientists last week, the universe is:

a. Missing.

b. Plaid.

c. No fun.

d. Leased from Donald Trump."

"Not everyone approves of his taste in design and architecture, but all agree that Trump knows how to build a quality building."

From *Boardroom Reports*, March 1, 1988

"Donald Trump epitomizes the new guard."

—Maggie Mahar—

THE BUILDING OF AN EMPIRE

Don King, the legendary boxing promoter with the reach-for-the-sky shock of hair, spoke fondly of Donald Trump, while Mr. Trump listened on. "Donald Trump is a man of vision," King said, "New York City needs a man like Donald Trump. I have come up with a word to describe him: 'telesynergistic.' That means, 'progress ingeniously planned by geometric progression—the capability of transforming dreams into living reality, in minimal time, at megaprofits.' "

Donald Trump's reaction? "Go on, Don, I kinda like this."

"Success brings success, which brings more success. The more he gets, the more he wants."
—Maryanne Trump-Barry—

Donald Trump was voted into an exalted third place in *Spy* magazine's, 1987, "100 Most Annoying, Alarming, and Appalling People, Places, and Things in New York and the Nation." First and second place winners in *Spy* magazine's list: Ivan Boesky and Ronald Reagan.

"Donald Trump, 41, is the glamour boy of the business, a self promoter who has recently been trumpeting his views on public policy in full-page newspaper ads that reek of political ambition."
—Barbara Hetzer, *Fortune*, 1987—

DONALD TRUMP

"Trump is no dummy when it comes to promotion. With drive, money, and a real estate man's eye for asset values, Trump appears to possess all the qualifications of a big league raider."
—Thomas Moore, *Fortune*, September, 1987—

"If you live in New York, you cannot not know Donald Trump."
—Barbara Walters, on charges that her interview subjects often are her personal friends—

"More than any developer of his generation . . . Donald J. Trump has succeeded over the last decade in reshaping the skyline of Manhattan. Taking advantage of political connections, a large family fortune and a salesman's aggressive optimism, he has effectively influenced the changing character of mid-town."
—Howard Blum, New York *Times*—

"Piggy. Piggy. Piggy."
—Mayor Ed Koch, on Trump for attempting to seek special New York City zoning, and large tax benefits—

"There's not a Republican running who can win the general election. I decided we better find someone who is capable of being elected."
—Mike Dunbar, founder of a "draft Donald Trump" movement, for the 1988 presidential election—

THE BUILDING OF AN EMPIRE

Often times, Donald Trump's name comes up in some very interesting places. In a humorous article by syndicated columnist Gerald Nachman which I found in the San Francisco *Chronicle*, the writer creatively designed a scenario with novelist and famed radio show host Garrison Keillor, living in the fast lane style of New York life. Mr. Nachman titled his piece, ''Happy to be Here in New Wobegon,'' and he couldn't help but to throw in a jab or two about Mr. Trump. And why not? The name Trump has spread into the far corners of America's awareness.

''Garrison Keillor, who just moved back to America after a sojourn in Sweden with his new Scandinavian bride, finally has settled in New York. His first report:

''It has been quite a week in New Wobegon, the little town that time forgot and that decadence cannot improve. Mayor Ed had some trouble down at City Hall, but nobody paid much notice. Lately, Mayor Ed just can't do much of anything right, but folks kinda dote on all the scandals, don'tcha know.

''A heap o' Ed's pals, includin' his lady friend Bessie, were indicted on some pretty fierce kickback schemes, but nothin' to get upset about. Down at Elaine's Chatterbox Bar & Grill, folks were saying as how the mayor might be run outta town, but they promptly forgot all about it 'cause of the new ducks-liver frittata that's the rage.

"The style page of our local paper, the New Wobegon *Times*, had a right nice write-up, and so folks hurried on over to give it a taste. Calvin Trillin, he had two helpings, so you knew it was pretty darn good.

"Last Sunday, a lot of folks like Calvin gathered over at Elaine's Chatterbox for the pre-Super Bowl polenta feed. My, how those folks in New Wobegon can put away that polenta! They musta ate clean through to Newark.

"I guess you could say everyone who mattered was there. I sat next to Georgie Plimpton, the writer fella, and way in the rear, under the Andy Warhol poster, was Mr. Woody Allen, who used to be a writer fella but is now a film-making genius fella, with his gal Mia. They had their new son, Satchel, along.

"Some folks think that Satchel's a pretty whimsical name for a kid, but this is a pretty whimsical town, unless you're from here. I'm a whimsical story-spinnin' fella myself, so naturally I was there, too.

"Pretty soon we all fell to talkin' about our agents. They got a lot of these agent folks in New Wobegon, and, my oh my, do they cause a ruckus when they all get to goin' at once—inkin' deals and holdin' paperback auctions and the like.

"Most writers in these parts have got some *real* amusin' tales to tell about their agents. I don't rightly recall any of 'em, but when they got through, why there wasn't a dry eye in the house.

"What else happened in New Wobegon? Let's see . . . Well, we had a close call on a transit strike, but they patched it up somehow, and our underground trolleys are runnin' again, if you can call that runnin'. Fact is, a body can make better time walkin', but on Sunday it's fun to take a nice leisurely ride on the IRT after church and see if you can get home again in one piece.

"That's one of the pastimes here, along with seein' who can wrestle a cab away from someone else. I lost a few of those cab-wrestlin' matches myself, but darned if it doesn't help pass the time between book signings and first nights."

In his development of Nachman's 'New Wobegon' for the article, he used the well known Trump name to make the feel of the city a little more real. Donald Trump has become a vital part of New York's mystique.

"I guess you might say the big talk here is all about Donny Trump—you know, that billionaire fella?

"Seems young Donny is tryin' to buy up the town, and Mayor Ed, well, he doesn't much like all the publicity that's been comin' Donny's way. Ed's a mite jealous about the media spotlight, as the locals call it.

"So the fur got to flyin' a few weeks ago, don'tcha know, when young Donny wanted to move one of our local broadcast outlets, NBC, over to the west side. That got Mayor Ed's back up somethin' awful, and they had words, but Donny backed off at the last minute. Young Donny sure does like to spend the bucks, though, largely to show up Mayor Ed.''

Gerald Nachman ended his article with, ''Guess that about wraps it up this week in New Wobegon, where all the men are powerful and unresponsive, the women are savvy, exciting, and slim, and the children are streetwise.''

''He's the sort of guy who, if he wants to go from New York to Atlanta, it takes 20 minutes. If you want to go—and he doesn't—it takes four hours.''

—Al Glasgow, *Barrons*, 1987—

''At a recent black-tie gala in the Resorts casino here, Donald Trump glided confidently among the guests, the undulating belly dancers, a costumed elephant, a turbaned fellow on a bed of nails, waiters bearing Dom Perignon. As he shook hands and kissed cheeks, the New York developer exuded the poise of a presidential candidate.''

—Julie Amparano, the *Wall Street Journal*, June 23, 1987—

''Energy is a word that frequently pops up in discussions about Donald Trump. Besides being a

fast talker, he is a fast walker, a fast eater, a fast business dealer, and gives the distinct impression of being an early candidate for a cardiac arrest.''
—Fred C. Trump, 1976—

"Donald's very demanding. He thinks nothing of calling me at 7 A.M. on Sunday saying, 'I've got an idea. See you in the office in 40 minutes.' And I always go. That Donald, he could sell sand to the Arabs and refrigerators to the Eskimos.''
—Der Scutt, architect on the convention center proposal, 1976—

"Trump is mad and wonderful. Other developers come in with sober faces, carrying their market-research studies on what the public will think.''
—Philip Johnson, architect—

"When I walk down the street with Donald, people come up and just touch him, hoping that his good fortune will rub off.''
—Blanche Sprague, Trump sales agent—

"He's got the uncanny ability to smell blood in the water.''
—anonymous competitor, *New York Times Magazine*, 1984—

"He captured the imagination of people to a greater degree than I could.''
—Preston Robert Tisch, developer—

"Donald Trump, is a transplanted 19th century swashbuckling entrepreneur, and it is up to public officials to rein him in. I don't so much fault him for asking the city for things as I do public officials who gave him his way."

—Henry J. Stern, city commissioner—

"He is an almost unbelievable negotiator. I don't worship at the shrine of Donald Trump, but our company has given up trying to negotiate with him. We just say: 'Tell us what you want, you're going to get it anyway.'"

—Irving Fischer, HHH Construction—

"He has an uncanny sense of knowing that something is a good deal when it looks dismal to everyone else."

—Roy M. Cohn—

"Anybody who succeeds at anything is likely to be the recipient of jealousy. Reporters who talk to me about Donald view him as a tough guy. That's not the case. I'm in the people business, and this man is a gentleman. Every time you try to compliment Donald, he diverts the praise to his father or mother. Donald is an honest genius who, in my humble judgment, will go down as one of the greatest builders of our era. Anything that Donald attempts, he's likely to succeed at."

—Rev. Norman Vincent Peale—

THE BUILDING OF AN EMPIRE

"When I want something, I want victory, completeness, results."

—Donald Trump—

"So I say to Donald Trump, hey, how 'bout spreadin' a little wealth over my way!!"

—Steve Dallas, former market investor—

Chapter 7
To the American People

"I don't know where the economy is going. I see Japan taking advantage of this country like I've never seen anything before. I see other countries taking advantage of the United States. So who knows where anybody's going to be over the next four or five years. Unless this country gets smart, and unless its leaders get smart, and they better damn well do it soon or this country is going to have some very big problems."

—Donald Trump—

On Wednesday, September 2, 1987, Donald Trump took out the following advertisement in major newspapers. The ad stated his views on the United States protecting foreign oil shipments in the Persian Gulf. Mr. Trump has always been an outspoken individual, and decided it was time to bring his ideas right to the American people.

"There's Nothing Wrong With America's Foreign Defense Policy that a Little Backbone Can't Cure.

"An open letter from Donald J. Trump on why America should stop paying to defend countries that can afford to defend themselves.

"To the American People:

"For decades now, Japan and other nations have been taking advantage of the United States.

The saga continues unabated as we defend the Persian Gulf, an area of only marginal significance to the United States for its oil supplies, but one upon which Japan and others are almost totally dependent. Why are these nations not paying the United States for the human lives and billions of dollars we are losing to protect *their* interests? Saudi Arabia, a country whose very existence is in the hands of the United States, last week refused to allow us to use their mine sweepers (which are, sadly, far more advanced than ours) to police the Gulf. The world is laughing at America's politicians as we protect ships we don't own, carrying oil we don't need, destined for allies who won't help.

Over the years, the Japanese, unimpeded by the huge costs of defending themselves (as long as the United States will do it for free), have built a strong and vibrant economy with unprecedented surpluses. They have brilliantly managed to maintain a weak yen against a strong dollar. This,

160

coupled with our monumental spending for their, and others, defense, has moved Japan to the forefront of world economies.

Now that the tides are turning and the yen is becoming strong against the dollar, the Japanese are openly complaining and, in typical fashion, our politicians are reacting to these unjustified complaints.

It's time for us to end *our* vast deficits by making Japan, and others who can afford it, pay. Our world protection is worth hundreds of billions of dollars to these countries, and their stake in *their* protection is far greater than ours.

"Make Japan, Saudi Arabia, and others pay for the protection we extend as allies. Let's help our farmers, our sick, our homeless by taking from some of the greatest profit machines ever created— machines created and nurtured by us. 'Tax' these wealthy nations, not America. End our huge deficits, reduce our taxes, and let America's economy grow unencumbered by the cost of defending those who can easily afford to pay us for the defense of their freedom. Let's not let our great country be laughed at anymore.

Sincerely, Donald J. Trump"

Not many Americans would spend so much of their own money, ($94,801) to save money for the rest of the country. To take such a bold stance as to come right out in the public forum and state a privately held view so forcefully. People have been tending to agree with Mr. Trump on most of this issue though, and the effect has spread.

The reaction to his paid advertisements has garnered Mr. Trump many a pat on the back, while causing others to take a cold and hard look at the situation that, up until the ads were taken, they hadn't really thought about. How do you tell the parents of a man aboard a U.S. ship that they're offering their young lives, when the Japanese seem to offer nothing in return? The situation must soon be dealt with to the mutual satisfaction of the U.S. and all of our allies. No one country should carry the burden of protection for any other. That is, however, exactly what America seems to be doing.

In a recent report by Iwao Nakatani, a professor of economics at Osaka University, and also the author of such books as *The Borderless Enemy*, and *The Japanese Firm In Transition*, some of the most widely sold publications of Japan's macroeconomics, on the subject of the United States' efforts in the tension filled Persian Gulf Nakatani wrote that the United States was in the process of what he called "Japan-bashing," and that the current feelings could possibly lead to the same tensions which led to the U.S. war with Japan in our recent past. "It is a truism," Nakatani said, "that Japan's economic growth since the war has been export-led. That is to say, this country's institutional arrangements are designed to promote the outflow of goods, capital, manpower, and enterprises to overseas markets—this is in stark contrast to the U.S. system which is highly import oriented. For this very reason a vast stream of Japanese goods, capital investments, and businesses is flowing into the United States.

"Suppose the United States does not take any effective action to curb its expanding deficit—or acts too late. The world economic system would then be certain to crack. What are the people of Japan supposed to think and do about this? Or what are they supposed not to do? Frankly speaking," Nakatani wrote, "many Japanese are now anxious and indeed almost at a loss to know which way to turn.

"Given the present atmosphere of 'Japan-bashing' in the United States, it would be most dangerous if the Japanese people were to allow themselves to get dragged into the sort of mass hysteria that prevailed on the eve of the war that Japan forced on the United States almost a half-century ago.

"The contention is often heard on the Japanese side that the present state of affairs is solely due to America's policy blunders, and that therefore the idea of the United States putting political pressure on Japan is thoroughly unreasonable and not to be tolerated. If, however, one asks whether there are no faults on the Japanese side, the answer can hardly be in the affirmative."

163

Nakatani then brought up the subject of the U.S. protecting Japanese and other foreign oil shipments. "The rise of Japan as an economic giant while the United States retains military and political power generates tensions that could eventually separate the two nations and drive them along divergent paths.

"The U.S. naval force in the Persian Gulf, for example, is protecting oil shipments that benefit Japan as much as any country. Japan has been criticized in Congress for failing to participate in the military action and, more generally, for spending only 1 percent of its gross national product on defense while the United States spends 6 percent.

"The Toshiba Corp., stopped selling high-tech equipment to the Soviet Union after the United States protested that the equipment benefitted the Russian military. The Japanese government even apologized, but some Japanese businessmen were angry that Japan backed down. They argued that Japan needs the Communist-bloc as a marketplace for its manufactured goods.

"But a policy that would incorporate such activities over the protests of the United States or other nations requires a sense of national mission and conviction that the Japanese prefer to avoid. Their reluctance stems from Japan's disastrous experience with militarism in the 1930's and 1940's and the strong Japanese sense of being apart from the rest of the world—a characteristic reinforced by the language barrier and by centuries of island isolation.''

Donald Trump didn't suggest that Japan build up its military might. He suggested that the United States simply charge them for our services offered. Other suggestions for clearing up this matter are to join into a pluralistic form of world government, in which each allied country shares responsibility. That, too, is not what Mr. Trump suggested. His idea is simple and could be executed in a matter of days. All that would need to be done is to refuse protection of these oil shipments, until Japan and the others paid for it.

During a recent television interview on Larry King's show, "Larry King Live," Mr. King asked Donald about the ads, and what kind of response he had been getting since they were published. "Oh, it was awesome," Mr. Trump responded happily. "It was tremendous. I took an ad, I said Japan and other countries, frankly, I'm using Japan as an example, but other countries are just ripping off the United States. And it's (the response) been just awesome, the reaction, and people agree with me. You don't have to be, uh, you don't have to see very clearly to see what's going on. It's a disgrace to this great country, what's happening.''

Mr. Trump, obviously dealing with a subject that he has strong feelings about, briefly explained his animosity. "You can't do business in Japan.

They come over here, they buy everything, they sell everything, they do whatever they want to do. You're over there, you can't do a thing. And it's a joke." Realizing that during the brief talk show interview, he's got to cover a lot of areas, Mr. Trump summed up the thought by sadly shaking his head and saying, "It's a total double standard. That's very unfortunate."

In an effort to further understand Donald Trump's letter to the American people, I contacted Mr. Paul Kullman, program coordinator for Great Decisions, the largest foreign policy study and discussion program in the United States. Great Decisions, '88, was an eight week meeting which follows 34 years of World Affairs Council's programs. The discussions cover the eight most important foreign affairs issues, per year, and Great Decisions, '88, was sponsored in part by the Foreign Policy Association, a non-government, nonpartisan organization. Its intent is to stimulate citizen participation in world affairs. The World Affairs Council, the Foreign Policy association, and the participants of Great Decisions, '88, recorded their interviews in opinion ballots that were distributed at the weekly meetings. The ballots were tabulated and circulated to congressional members and the executive branch.

I spoke to Mr. Kullman during the week of "U.S. Trade and Global Markets: Risks and Opportunities" conference, and asked for his views.

Taking time from the pressures of the World Affairs' briefings, Mr. Kullman responded after our telephone conversation by special courier.

"Regarding Mr. Trump's letter," Mr. Kullman told me, "I agree with his general premise that those countries able to afford, but unable to provide their own defense, should contribute more to the U.S. armed forces. The United States and its allies will have to agree on their perceptions on the kinds of threats and the degree of threat in the international arena. U.S. protection will also have to be found the most beneficial means of furthering their own interests.

"If this be the case," he told me, "one could say that these countries are 'hiring' the United States to protect them and their interests around the world. These countries that support the U.S. military, and to some degree political sovereignty may be decreased, but the increased cooperation with our allies will tie us closer together making all of us, ultimately, stronger.

"The United States puts itself into the current position of the world's policeman, no one else. Now when the United States is having difficulty paying for its role, it is whining and screaming at its allies. This won't do. We must cooperate."

The day Mr. Kullman sent me his views, I talked to him again on the phone. He told me that he'd sent the material, but wondered if I could use what he wrote in the book because "it wasn't all good." I assured him that I would use his opinions in the book, whether they were good or bad.

"I would like to take issue on a few specific points made in the letter," he said in his response. "Regarding the Persian Gulf, I do not believe that the United States is presently risking a war for the sake of the oil supplies (of which only one percent was hampered by the Iran-Iraq war) or the idea of freedom of navigation. The main point of U.S. intervention is to make sure that Iran does not overrun Iraq. That possibility was all the more prevalent after the shipment of tons of U.S. military equipment. If Iraq lost, our oil supplies would truly be at risk, anti-Western sentiments and terrorism would be on the rise and Israel would be in grave danger of another war.

"Concerning the sentence, 'The (the Japanese) have brilliantly managed to maintain a weak Yen against a strong dollar,' I believe this no longer holds true as the strong Yen indicates. But at the time of Mr. Trump's letter and during many years prior to that, the United States had tremendously high interest rates which boosted the value of the dollar. The Japanese didn't have to be so brilliant to maintain a weak Yen!

"The final issue I would like to consider is the solution offered by Mr. Trump. We all want to cut the deficit, reduce taxes and let America's economy grow, but simply 'taxing' other countries is not going to do it. We must also look at ourselves.

Some belt-tightening on our own part, a possible rise in taxes and maybe more government involvement, like we see in Japan and West Germany, in planning may make this country's economy more effective.

"All empires rise and, eventually, fall," Mr. Kullman said, summing up his feelings. "The United States has reached and passed its zenith and now must come to grips with not being a superpower, but a country that is first among equals. Simply blaming others, while not being prepared to deal with one's own internal problems, will only speed up the process of the *Falling of an Empire.*"

Some saw Donald Trump's ads as a way to begin hinting at a political beginning on his part. In an article in the Los Angeles *Times*, Trump's possible candidacy was a mentioned concern to writer, Michael A. Hiltzik. Hiltzik wrote that Trump, "Maneuvered himself into a brief spot in the national political limelight by journeying up to New Hampshire late last year to give a speech on, of all things, foreign policy.

"Trump's theme," Hiltzik recounted, "articulated simultaneously in full page ads in the New York *Times* and Boston *Globe,* was that America should force its rich partners, including Japan, to pay for the military protection they receive from U.S. armed forces.

"Back in New York," the writer continued,

"he luxuriated in the speculation that he might run for public office.

" 'I went to New Hampshire,' he remarked during an interview, 'and—you know what happened —we had the biggest reception of anybody. The fact is, I really agreed to do it for a friend, and simultaneously I took an ad which had nothing to do with the trip . . . and people started saying: the ad, New Hampshire . . . Is Donald Trump going to be running for president?' "

Reminded that, given the dynamics of American politics, any such activity in or around New Hampshire within a year or two of a presidential election has the appearance of politicking, Trump assumes an ingenuous and transparent look of surprise and says: "You know what? I just found that out!"

A caller on the Larry King Live show, asked Donald Trump, ". . . Let's say that over the next five years you should attain a wealth of $10 to $15 billion dollars, would you be satisfied at this point in life, with what you've done? Or is it fame and fortune you're really after?"

Trump responded, "It's really more of an asthetic quality than it is anything else. I love what I do. I don't do it for the money. If I did it for the money perhaps I wouldn't do so well. Uh, I'm flattered by the $15 billion dollars . . . that would be pretty good. But, because I don't know where the world is going, I don't know where the economy is going. I see Japan taking advantage of this country like I've never seen anything before. I see other countries taking advantage of the United States. So who knows where anybody's going to be over the next four or five years, unless this country gets smart, and unless its leaders get smart, and they better damn well do it soon or this country is going to have some very big problems.''

When asked if he thought that some of the financial problems facing the United States were caused in part by corporate greed, Mr. Trump responded, ''Well, I think there's a certain amount of greed. I guess, unfortunately, greed's a familiar word to everybody, whether it's corporations or individuals. The fact is that I believe the biggest problem this country has, isn't with the corporations within the country, it's really with the countries outside of this country. We have tremendous competition, with government subsidies and everything else, competing against our great companies, and I just hope we get smart to what's happening before it's too late. It's a real big problem. I don't like to use the word greed, but I'd like to see our companies get more competitive than they are. And if they did, we have the people to do it. If they did, we'd beat the world, and that's what I'd like to see.''

Bibliography

BOOKS:

Hammer, Armand. *Hammer,* G. P. Putnam & Sons, N.Y.

Musashi, Miyamoto. *The Book of Five Rings,* Bantam Books, 1982.

Rosenbaum, Ron. *Manhattan Passions,* Beachtree Books.

Trump, Donald. *The Art of the Deal,* Random House, 1987.

NEWSPAPERS & PERIODICALS:

Amparano, Julie. "Donald Trump on a roll on Atlantic City," *The Wall Street Journal.* (June 23, 1987).

Amparano, Julie. "New Jersey Gives Trump Clearance to Run Taj Mahal," *The Wall Street Journal,* (July 3, 1987).

Allen, Frank. "Officer at Trump's Casino is facing kickback charges," *The Wall Street Journal,* (Sept. 29, 1987).

Belis, Gary. "Donald Trump Explained," *Fortune* (Jan. 4, 1988).

Blum, Howard, "Trump: The Development of a Manhattan Developer," The New York *Times* (Aug. 26, 1980).

Boyle, Robert. "The USFL's Trump Card," *Sports Illustrated* (date unknown)

Benway, Susan & Teu, Lawrence. "Donald Trump gets a $200 million Christmas gift," *Business Week* (Dec. 28, 1987).

Barnathan, Joyce and Shwartz, John. "Trump lands in Red Square," *Newsweek* (July 20, 1987).

Bock, Gordon, Griggshee & McDowell, Jeanne. "Air Pockets Around United," *Time* (April 20, 1987).

Cohen, Laurie. "Trump to launch tender offer for rest of Resorts International's class B Stock," *The Wall Street Journal* (Oct. 28, 1987).

Dunlap, David. "Anti-Peddler Drive Pleases Fifth Ave. Merchants," The New York *Times* (Jan. 6, 1987).

Delugach, Al. "Trump's interest behind run up in MCA stock," Los Angeles *Times* (Feb. 17, 1988).

Eklund, Christopher & Oneal, Michael. "For Bally, Dumping Trump Raises the Ante," *Business Week* (March 9, 1987).

Fromartz, Samuel. "Icahn, Texico President differ on sale discussions." *The Examiner* (Jan. 20, 1988).

Flanigan, James. "Trump finds the real glitter of Hollywood," Los Angeles *Times* (Feb. 17, 1988).

Fiske, Jack. "The Man with the golden arm rolls eleven," San Francisco *Chronicle* (Feb. 27, 1988).

Geist, William E. "The expanding empire of Donald Trump," *New York Times Magazine* (April 8, 1984)

Grover, Ronald & Norman, James. "Trump vs Wynn: Giant egos on the line," *Business Week* (July 27, 1987).

Hetzer, Barbara. "Where are the Duponts?" *Fortune* (Oct. 12, 1987).

Hiltzik, Michael A. "N.Y.'s Landlord may be shopping on the west coast," Los Angeles *Times* (Feb. 28, 1988).

Klemesrud, Judy. "Donald Trump, Real Estate Promoter builds image as he buys buildings," The New York *Times* (Nov. 1, 1976).

Lowenstein, Roger. "Trump says he purchased a 4.9% stake in Golden Nugget, Indicates possible Bid," *The Wall Street Journal* (July 9, 1987).

Lowenstein, Roger. "Mayor Koch spurns Trump's bid to get sweeping tax breaks for New York Site," *The Wall Street Journal* (Date Unknown).

Lowenstein, Roger. "New York fights to keep NBC in town as Real-Estate suitors woo network," *The Wall Street Journal* (1987).

McKillop, Peter & Powel, Bill. "Citizen Trump," *Newsweek* (Sept. 28, 1987).

Moore, Thomas. "How the 12 Top Raiders rate," *Fortune* (Sept. 28, 1987).

Mahar, Maggie. "Here come the high rollers," *Barron's* (April 13, 1987).

Meagher, James P. "A Suburban Mall in Manhattan?" *Barron's* (July 21, 1986).

Marcus, Adrianne. "A food lover's tour of New York," The San Francisco *Chronicle* (Jan. 27, 1988).

Norman, James R. "Trump—What's Behind the hype?" *Business Week* (July 20, 1987).

Nachman, Gerald. "Happy to be here in New Wobegon," The San Francisco *Chronicle* (Jan. 26, 1988).

Nakatani, Iwao. "How Japanese view their new leadership role," The San Francisco *Chronicle* (Feb. 10, 1988).

Obeskes, Michael. "Trump Gives a Vague Hint of Candidacy," The New York *Times* (Sept. 2, 1987).

Pearson, Hunter. "Laxalt, Libel and Liberals," *Mother Jones* (Jan. 16, 1987).

Smith, Randall. "Ace Developer Donald Trump builds a Real Estate Empire using Loans, Contacts," "The Tax Deal of the Century," *The Wall Street Journal* (Jan. 14, 1982).

Schwartz, John, Wang, Penelope & McKillop, Peter. "Donald Trump's Mystery," *Newsweek* (June 29, 1987).

Ticer, Scott. "Holiday Tries to Bar the Door Against Trump," *Business Week* (Nov. 24, 1986).

Trump, Donald. "No One Knows What's Going to Happen," *The Wall Street Journal* (Oct. 2, 1987).

Uchitelle, Louis. "Japan Resists Wielding Economic Might," The San Francisco *Chronicle* (Feb. 10, 1988).

Yardley, Jonathan. "Donald Trump's big sale," The *Orange County Register* (Jan. 3, 1988).

AUTHORS UNKNOWN:

•"Trump and Interstate Properties End Talks to buy Alexander's," *The Wall Street Journal* (Sept. 29, 1987).

•"Golden Nugget Inc," *The Wall Street Journal* (Sept. 4, 1987).

THE BUILDING OF AN EMPIRE

- "Pan Am Corp. Shares Rise on Report of Trump Stake," *The Wall Street Journal* (June 9, 1987).
- "Court Clears Trump's Bid for Resorts International," *The Wall Street Journal* (June 10, 1987).
- "Making sense out of Foreign Policy", San Francisco *Chronicle* (Jan. 27, 1988).
- "Resorts International Inc. Angered Some Holders by Boosting the Annual Salary of its Chief Executive Officer," *The Wall Street Journal* (June 8, 1987).
- "Donald Trump Says Red Tape Ruined NBC Project," United Press International, The San Francisco *Chronicle* (Oct. 31, 1987).
- "New Limos Have Built-in Shredders," The San Francisco *Chronicle* (Jan. 13, 1988).
- "Donald Trump's Circus and Bread," The New York *Times* (Nov. 9, 1987).
- "Trump, The Saga of America's Most Powerful Real Estate Baron," (May 10, 1985).
- "Men Who Made a Difference," *Professional Builder* (April 1986).
- "Trump May Buy the Patriots," The San Francisco *Chronicle* (Feb. 18, 1988).
- "Secrets of Trump's Success, What His Book Doesn't Tell," *Boardroom Reports* (March 1, 1988), Vol. 17, No. 5.

MISC:

Trump, Donald. "There's nothing wrong with America's Foreign Defense Policy that a little backbone can't cure." Paid Advertisement, The New York *Times* (Sept. 2, 1987).

DONALD TRUMP

Trump, Donald. "Ridiculous Award," Letter to the Editor, The New York *Times* (May 1, 1987).

Simmons, Matty. "Editorial," *National Lampoon* (Feb. 1988).

"Bloom County," © 1988 Washington Post Writers Group, Steve Dallas © 1988, Breathed, W.P.W.G., (Feb. 21, 1988).

TELEVISION:

"Larry King Live" —Interview with Donald Trump, CNN News Network (Feb. 3, 1988).

REFERENCE:

Current Biography Yearbook, Trump, Donald J.(ohn), (1984).

"I just do it for the enjoyment. I do it for the asthetic quality . . . if it's building, whether it's deals, whatever it might be, I love doing it beautifully. I love doing it like a picture, and a deal can be a picture just like a building can be a picture. My buildings have been, you know, the best buildings in the best locations, and that's what I love. My deals have been very good."

—Donald John Trump, 1988—